Lotte JACOBI
PHOTOGRAPHS

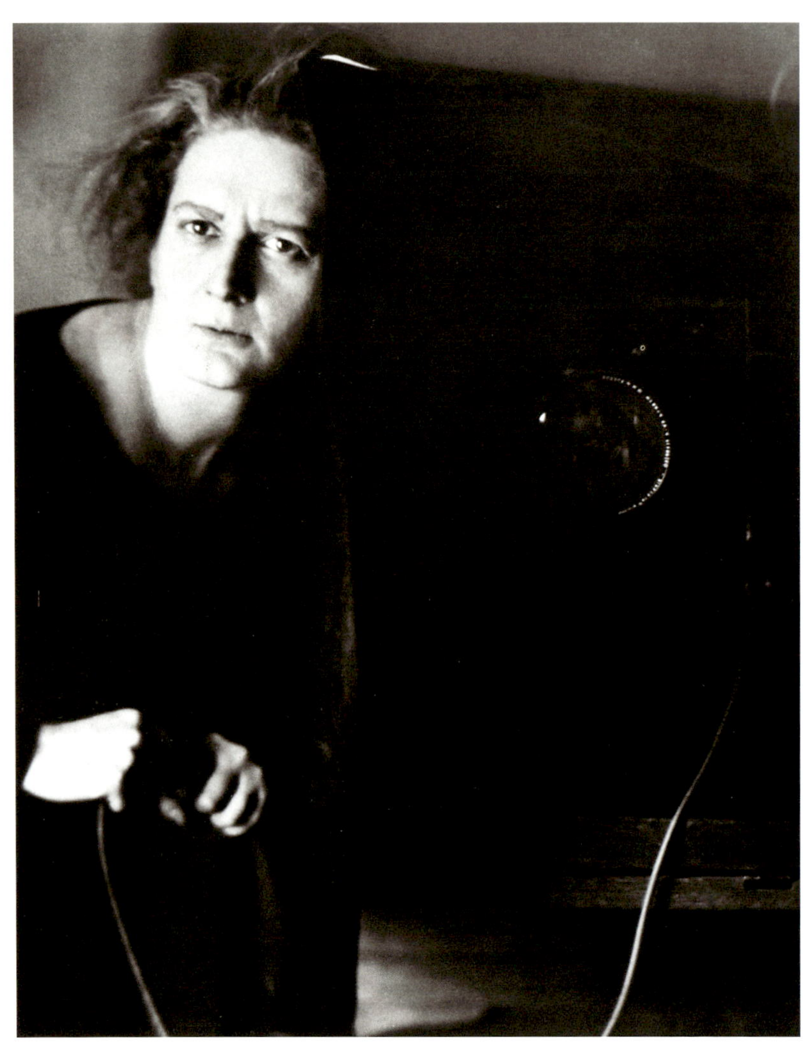

Self-Portrait, Berlin, c. 1929

LOTTE JACOBI
PHOTOGRAPHS

INTRODUCTION
AND NOTES BY
PETER MORIARTY

A POCKET PARAGON BOOK

DAVID R. GODINE
PUBLISHER · BOSTON

A GODINE POCKET PARAGON
first published in 2003 by
DAVID R. GODINE, *Publisher*
Post Office Box 450
Jaffrey, New Hampshire 03452
www.godine.com

Opposite: Studio card of Alexander Jacobi.

LIBRARY OF CONGRESS
CATALOGING-IN-PUBLICATION DATA
Jacobi, Lotte, 1896–1990
Lotte Jacobi : photographs /
introduction and notes by Peter Moriarty.— 1st ed.
          p. cm.
ISBN 1–56792–152–3 (alk. paper)
1. Portrait photography. I. Moriarty, Peter A. II. Title.

TR680.J3197 2002
779'.092–dc21   2002026411

FIRST EDITION 2003
Printed in Iceland by Oddi Printing

Introduction

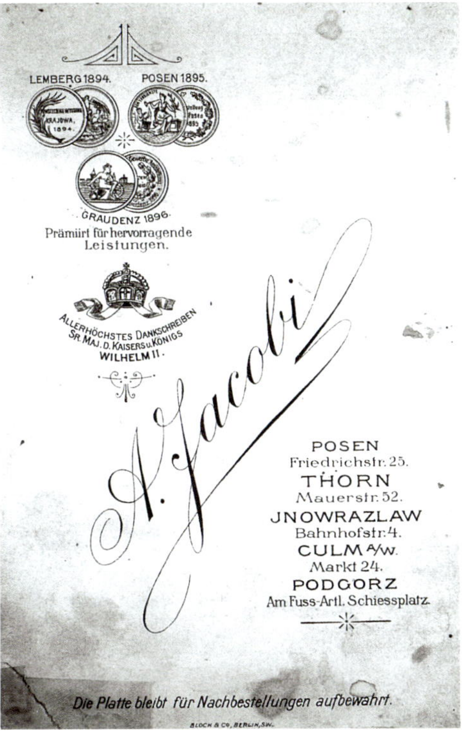

When I was about that age to make a decision [about the course of my life] I did not want to be a photographer. I said, "Three generations is enough! You know as young people do not want anything to do with what their parents have done." [1]

WE ARE FORTUNATE that Lotte Jacobi did not maintain her adolescent stance about her future. Her father Sigismund, her grandfather Alexander, and her great grandfather Samuel had all been photographers. She had thought that she might become an actor, a beekeeper, or a gardener rather than continue as a fourth-generation Jacobi photographer.

Her career, played out on both sides of the Atlantic Ocean, would span seven decades and embrace several cultures. With her camera she recorded the vibrant Weimar culture in Berlin before Adolf Hitler came to power in the spring of 1933. She photographed the USSR at a precarious time (1932–33) in world history. She portrayed significant artists, scientists, and men and women of letters who had escaped the chaos of Europe during the Second World War and had immigrated to the United States. She exhibited the work of artists within her New York and New Hampshire studios. She was central in the revival of the photogenic drawing as a form of photographic expression in the mid-1940s. In the last third of her life she did manage to work as a gardener, a beekeeper, a politician, and a mentor to young people, but she also engaged us through the creation of a dynamic photographic œuvre.

She was a humanist rather than a formalist. Her camera sought out the people she valued and to whom the world would pay attention.

JOHANNA ALEXANDRA JACOBI was born August 17, 1896, in Thorn, West Prussia. Within two years her family moved to Posen, Germany, which after 1918 became the Polish town Poznan. In 1920 the family moved again, this time to Berlin. Her father was

Sigismund and her mother's given name was Marie Lublinski, but Lotte called her Oëms. Lotte was the eldest of three children. Her sister, Ruth Jacobi-Roth (1899–1995), was also a photographer and she had a brother, Alexander (1902–c. 1922).

When asked about her great grandfather, Samuel, who went to Paris (c. 1840) and met Louis-Jacques Mandé Daguerre, the principal European inventor of photography, she replied, "[He] went to Paris with three other people from different parts of Germany and there they encountered that new thing, Daguerre's photography. Each [person] bought a camera and a license. They were instructed by him. Talked. You know how that is?"[2] When Samuel returned to Posen and started to make daguerreotypes, townspeople would say, "Let's go down town and have a Jacobi taken."[3] Thus the Jacobi name was interwoven from early on with the art and practice of making photographic portraits.

In 1916 Lotte made an unfortunate marriage to Fritz Honig. After a period of separation she returned to him, became pregnant, and gave birth to her only child, Jochen in 1917, who later anglicized his name to John F. Hunter when he went to England. One incident she remembered demonstrates the difference in personality between Jacobi and Honig: "A new person had been hired to clean their house. When she had finished Fritz put on a white glove, ran it along the mantel, and displayed the soiled finger. Lotte looked at him, said nothing, reached into the closet and handed him a dust rag."[4]

By 1921, Lotte was no longer with Fritz and was working at her father's Berlin studio, studying the finer points of photography and taking care of her son, who spent considerable time with the Jacobi family. By 1925, she decided to formally begin a career and she enrolled at the Bavarian State Academy of Photography where she studied until 1927.

In addition to taking courses in still photography she also

learned motion picture film technique and this study of film became important to her stylistic evolution as a still photographer. Film-making meant dealing with people who were working on a schedule. Jacobi had to work quickly as the tempo of their acting affected the creative process. This filmmaking experience carried over to her style of portraiture. Whether using a tripod-mounted studio camera or her smaller Ermanox or Leica cameras, she was quicker to respond to the expressions of her sitters than was typical at this time in photography. At the University of Munich she also studied the history of art before assuming responsibility for her father's Jacobi Atelier in Berlin, 1927.

Jacobi never felt constrained within her family for being born a woman. Her family contradicted the stereotype of stern nineteenth-century Prussian parents; its style was rather bohemian in character. Evidence of their free and curious approach to people and culture can be found in a solo pleasure trip Lotte's mother made to the USSR in the 1920s. Oëms traveled alone in that vast land, at one point waiting days for a train, sleeping with her luggage. A lone woman's journey in an unstable, post-revolutionary Russia[5] was a true adventure, and her fearless embrace of the world is a trait her daughter Lotte inherited.

Lisl Karlstadt and Karl Valentin, *Comedians, Berlin, c. 1930*

Weimar Portraits

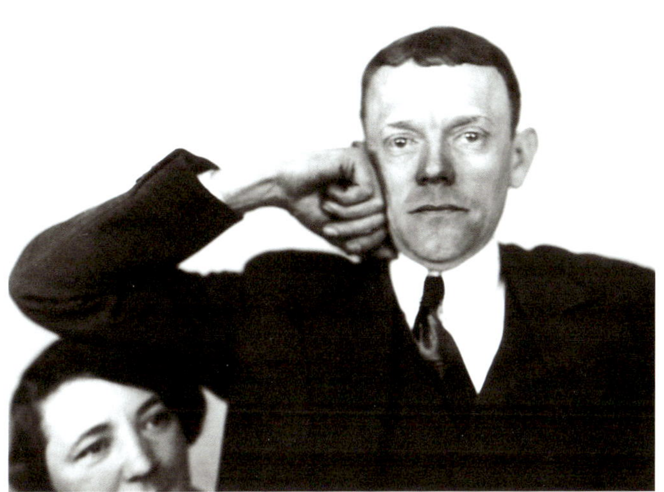

ONE OF Jacobi's key contributions to history was her photographic portraits of key personalities of Weimar culture in the years before Hitler assumed power. The atrocities of World War II and the destruction of her Berlin archive by the Nazis jeopardized this seminal work. Fortunately, Otto Steinert reversed this trend by exhibiting and publishing her work at the Folkwang Museum in Essen, Germany, in 1973 and 1974.

The poignant and relaxed portrait of Martin Buber, Odenwald (1928) is an early indication of her gift. He leans gently to the right, seemingly unaware of Lotte's gaze. As viewers we feel intimacy with the renowned theologian, who had published his seminal text, *I and Thou* in 1923. The whimsical double portrait of Karl Valentin and Lisl Karlstadt (*c.* 1930) reveals another facet of the Weimar culture. The comedians are spoofing the male dominance of women and Lotte's intuitive camera work has recorded their witty gesture and overlapping forms. Germany had its own women's movement in the 1920s and Jacobi was hardly surprised when America faced the same issues some fifty years later.

The insouciant portrait of Lotte Lenya embodies the qualities of the new woman. Her provocative stare provides a hint of the louche world of the cabaret where she was working as a singer and performer. When Jacobi made this Berlin portrait in 1930, Lenya was married to Kurt Weill, composer of *The Threepenny Opera* in which she performed so memorably. The culture of the cabarets created new art forms, explored diverse sex roles and tested the limits of alcohol consumption. When the Nazi spectre darkened this avant-garde culture, the words Bolshevik, Jew, and homosexual became linked in the most derogatory way. In a terse statement about the decline of the Weimar culture Jacobi observed, "People lost their jobs and became hungry and the Germans have always liked uniforms."[6]

Another facet of Lotte's œuvre is her many wonderful photographs of dancers. The significance of these pictures was immediately recognized by curators. They were included in *La Danse et le Mouvement: Exposition Internationale de Photographie* in Paris (1933–1934). One of her favorite subjects was Pauline Koner, a dancer who hoped to express "intrinsic dance, basic, essential, organic, internal — as opposed to extrinsic, the kind of dance that is imposed from outside."[7] Koner compared her aspirations within dance to the universal language expressed in Käthe Kollwitz's lithographs, "which have a tremendous sense of pathos and compassion for the human being. It is conveyed in the feeling of the body line."[8] Lotte photographed Koner both in Berlin and New York. In one print Lotte combined a negative of her dancing with an abstract shape added later in the darkroom. Lotte's cameraless light drawing extended the line Koner had created on stage.

Jacobi's dance photographs are beautifully free responses to light, movement and form. Niura Norskaya was dancing with Anna Pavlova at the time her picture, often titled *The Head of a Dancer*, was taken.[9] The sweeping curves of an oversized black hat contrast with Norskaya's bright, simplified features. She gleams at us like a modern porcelain doll.

General Kurt von Schleicher was a career officer and diplomat who tried to reconcile the differences between the Prussian government and the Reich. From December 3, 1932, to January 28, 1933, he served as the last chancellor of the Weimar Republic. In an effort to forestall the National Socialist movement he offered the position of vice-chancellor to Hitler, who refused this limited role in the transitional Schleicher government.

Jacobi's photograph of Schleicher in Berlin captures a fleeting moment in the life of a pivotal character in the collapsing Weimar Republic. It also suggests her willingness to work for a political purpose. On June 30, 1934, Hitler's SS murdered approximately eighty-five people in a purge referred to as the Night of the Long Knives.

Schleicher, his wife, and Ernst Roehm were among the victims; they were denounced as sexual deviants and traitors to the state.

THROUGHOUT HER CAREER Lotte made photographs that reflected her leftist social and political views — a stance that often adds a new dimension to her pictures, placing them beyond the superficiality of conventional celebrity portraits. While business referrals to the Jacobi Atelier in Berlin ensured a steady stream of customers, the most interesting portraits in the Jacobi catalogue are those of people whom Jacobi valued for their sense of social responsibility. Those people were censored, considered degenerate, forced into exile, or murdered by the Nazi regime.

One example, the introspective visage of the painter and sculptor Käthe Kollwitz (1929), seems familiar to us because she so often included an image of herself in her work, an expression of profound empathy for the plight of the German people. On May 15, 1933 Kollwitz was forced to resign her post as director of graphic arts at the Prussian Academy of Arts where she had been working as the first female professor since 1919. The Nazi regime was suspicious of her support of the Communist Workers Movement. Although she was a non-Jewish artist, an exhibition of her work was banned in 1936 as a result of her objections to the regressive climate in Germany. Despite this public censorship Albert Speer, the architect for Hitler's regime, had a Kollwitz print, *La Carmagnole,* on his bedroom wall. "It showed a howling mob dancing with hate-contoured faces around a guillotine. Off to the side a weeping woman, cowering on the ground."[10]

There is evidence that Tina Modotti — in exile from Mexico and en route to the USSR — visited Jacobi in Berlin while on a six-month visa in 1930. Modotti struggled to establish herself as a photographer in Berlin. In the archives at the University of New Hampshire is an Edward Weston portrait of Modotti, *Tina, Tacubaya,*

1923, that bears the stamp of the leftist Berlin Unionbild (Union Photo agency) on the reverse. The mark indicates that Modotti used the print in her search for work. Her use of the print as a latter-day *carte-de-visite* is a notable departure from Weston's aesthetic intention for the portrait. Jacobi exhibited Modotti's own work at her studio during the visit. When asked about Modotti's involvement with Edward Weston, Jacobi insisted that their affair was not a proper topic for public discussion, but said, "Tina taught Edward as much as Edward taught Tina. Not in photography, but in life."[11] Jacobi owned a Modotti print, *Indio Boy, Mexico City*, that is further evidence of exchanges between two women who valued photography's power to effect social change. This print appeared in *A Photographer's Photographs* (1974) at the Currier Gallery of Art in Manchester, New Hampshire, which exhibited Lotte's collection.

From August 1932 to February 1933 Lotte traveled to remote areas of the the USSR. She had photographed Ernest Thalmann, the Communist party candidate for the presidency of Germany in 1932, and was given the trip as a barter exchange for her photographs. Jacobi visited Modotti in Moscow and found that Modotti's revolutionary and political activities had taken precedence over her photographic projects.

By March of 1933 Adolf Hitler's National Socialist government was firmly in place. An indication of the dual peril that Jacobi faced at this moment in

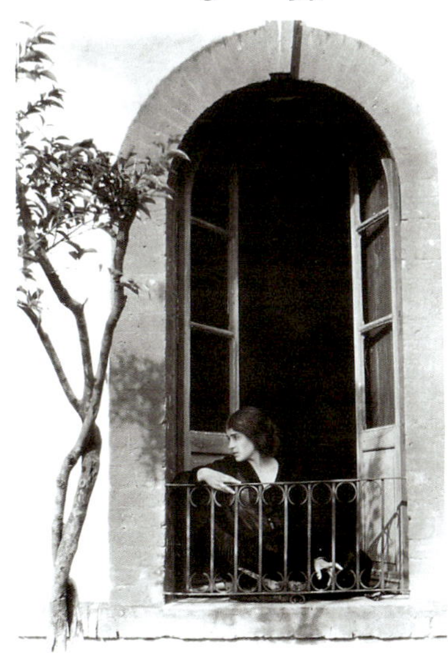

Tina, Tacubaya, *1923*
Photograph by Edward Weston

her life can be found in the fate of Thalmann. "Ernst Thalmann is tracked down and arrested in a hiding place in the Charlottenburg section of Berlin. He never regains his freedom. After eleven years of solitary confinement in various prisons, he is taken to the Buchenwald concentration camp in August, 1944 and murdered there."[12]

Lotte's mother contacted her in the the U S S R and warned her that the Gestapo might be waiting for her at customs. Alert to this warning, she bought a large, curvaceous fur coat, wore it, hid her cameras, and walked right by the Gestapo. They were looking for a photographer wearing a torn leather jacket. What they saw was a rich tourist.[13] In view of the headlines continually warning the German public against a Jewish and Bolshevist Revolution in order to bolster support for the Nazi regime, it was amazing that Lotte was never detained or imprisoned. The writing was on the wall; her time in Germany was coming to a close.

Lotte's Jewish heritage (on the part of both her parents) and her identification with figures of the political left placed her life in great peril during the upheaval Germany experienced in the 1930s. She was implicated in every possible way with the political left; as early as 1929 she photographed the anarchist poet, Erich Mühsam, who was murdered by the Nazis on July 11, 1934 in the Oranien-burg concentration camp. The journalist Egon Erwin Kisch, a friend Lotte had photographed in Moscow and Berlin, was arrested for cultural Bolshevism on February 28, 1933 — the day after the Reichstag fire — and incarcerated at Spandau for a brief period.

Sigismund, Lotte's father, was ill when the Nazis came to power. Even though he was a Jew, he considered himself — as did many of his assassinated countrymen — to be a German first and so insisted he be allowed to die in his homeland. After his death due to natural causes, Lotte was able to plan her departure from Nazi Germany.

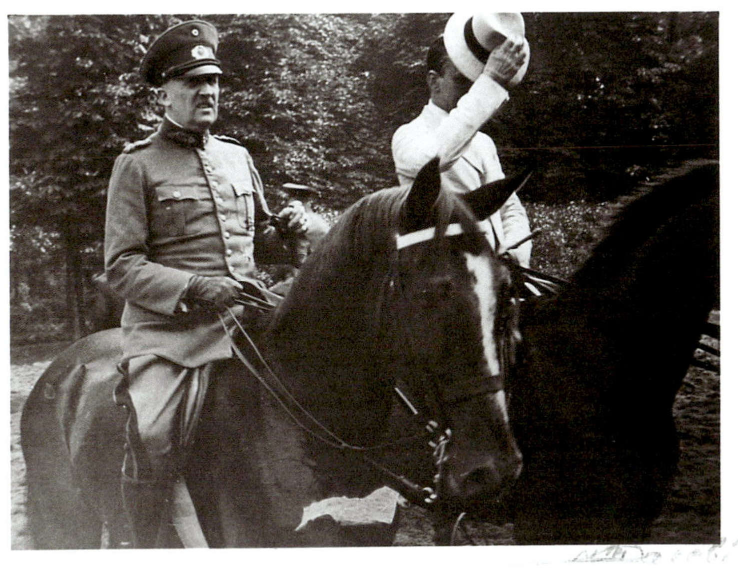

General Kurt von Schleicher, *Berlin, c. 1930*

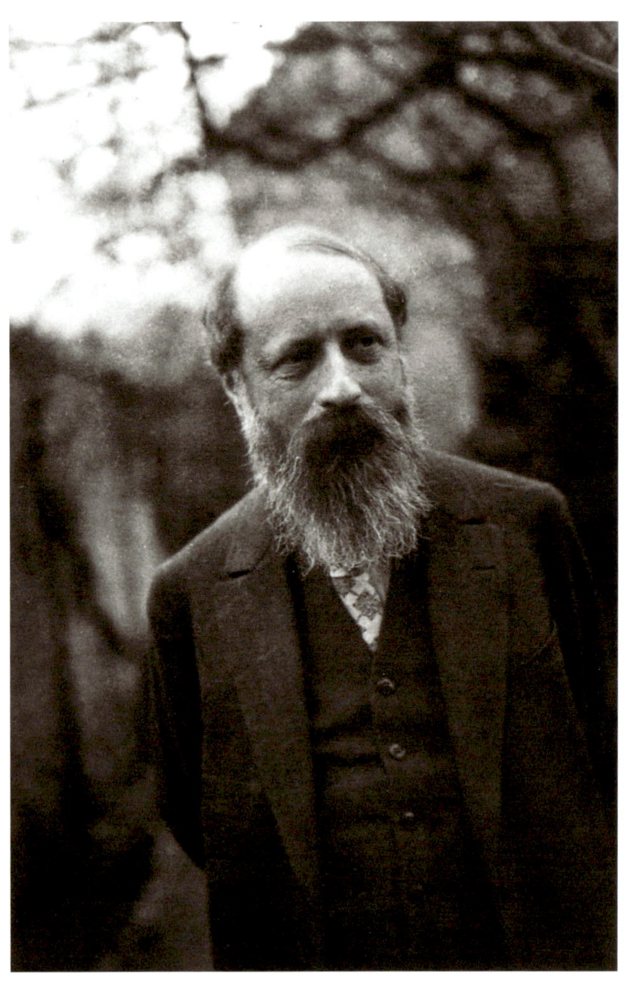

Martin Buber, *Theologian, Odenwald, 1928*

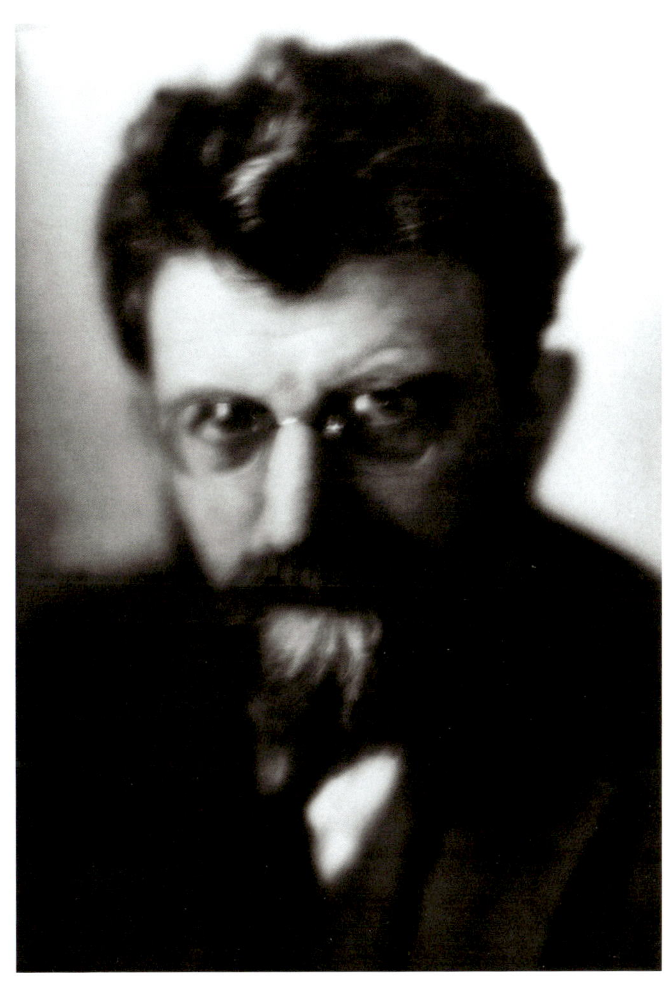

Eric Mühsam, *Poet, 1929*

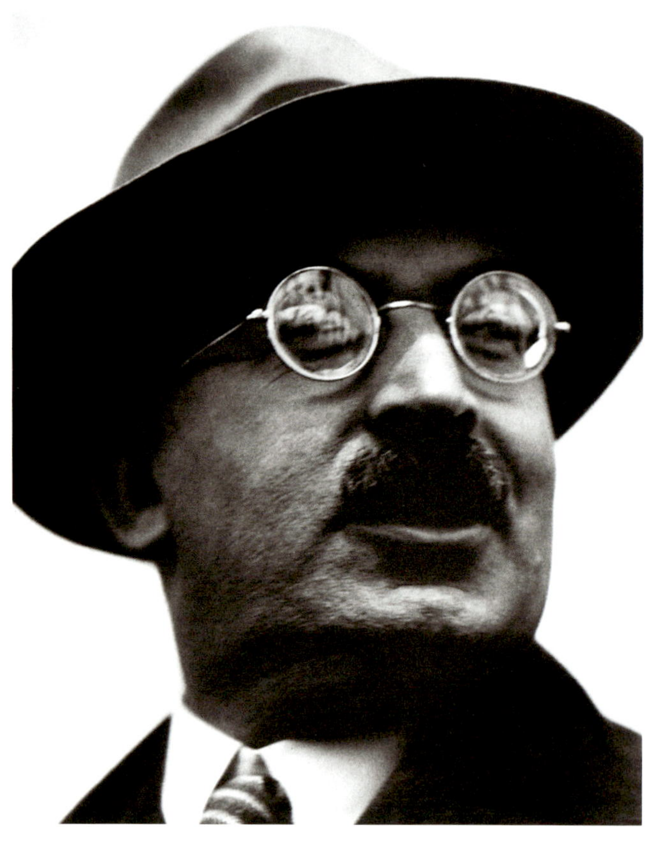

Arnold Zweig, *Writer, Berlin, c. 1930*

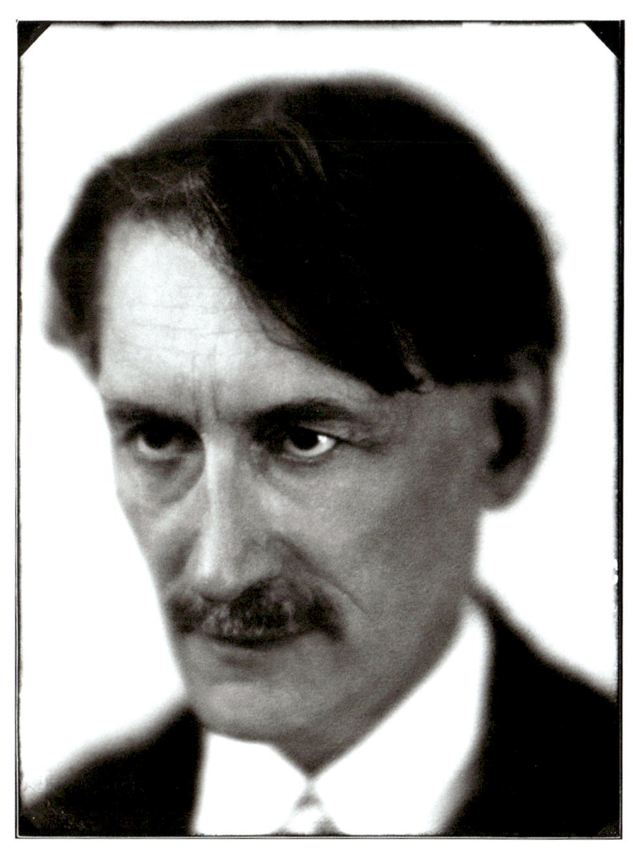

Henri Barbusse, *Writer, Berlin, 1930*

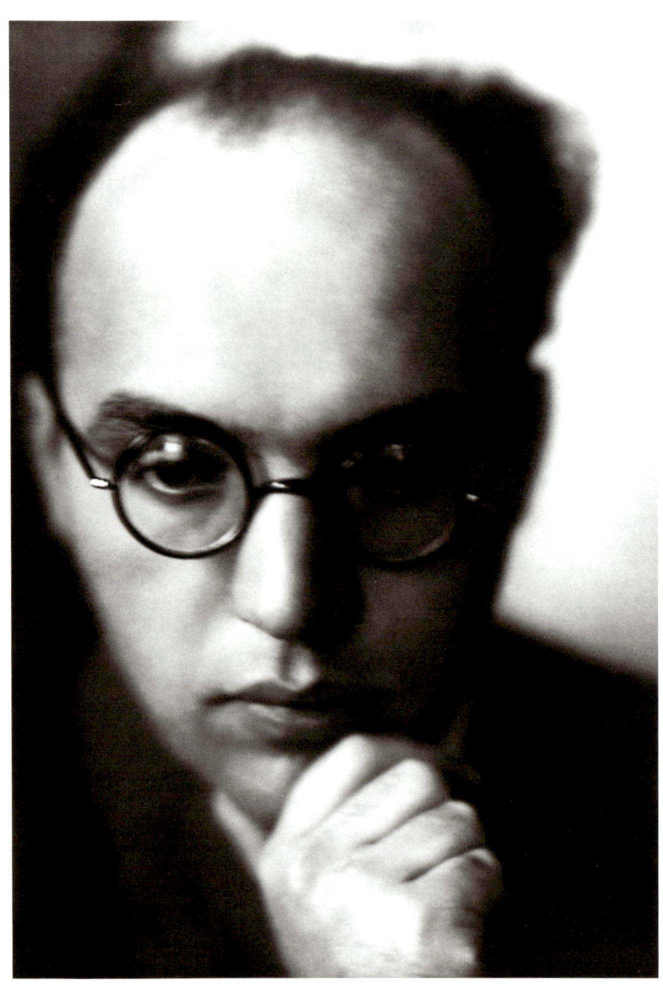

Kurt Weill, *Composer, Germany, 1928*

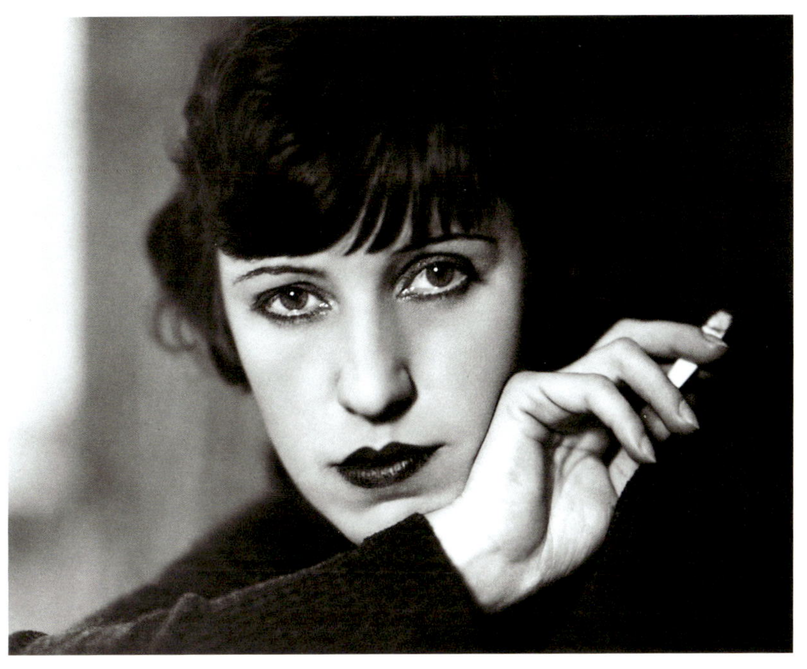

Lotte Lenya, *Actress, Berlin, c. 1930*

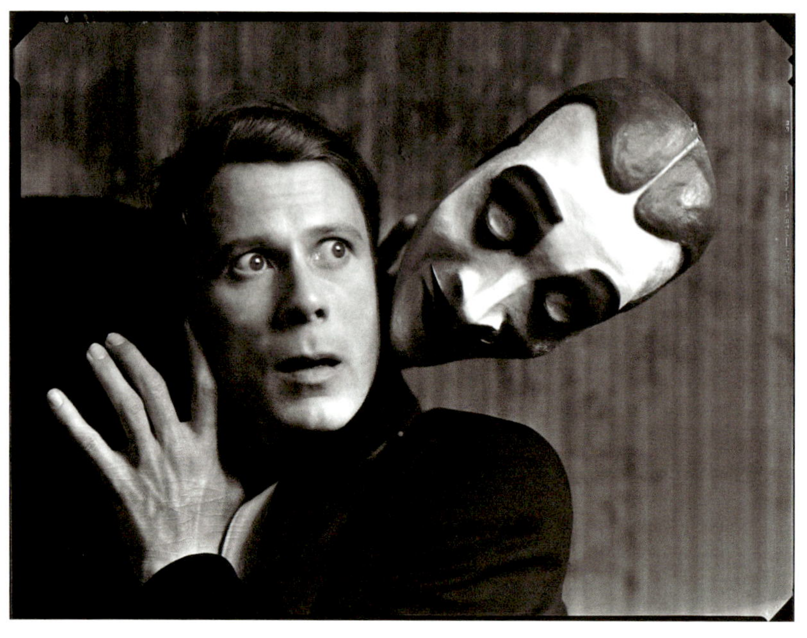

Rolf Arno, *Dancer, Berlin, c. 1930*

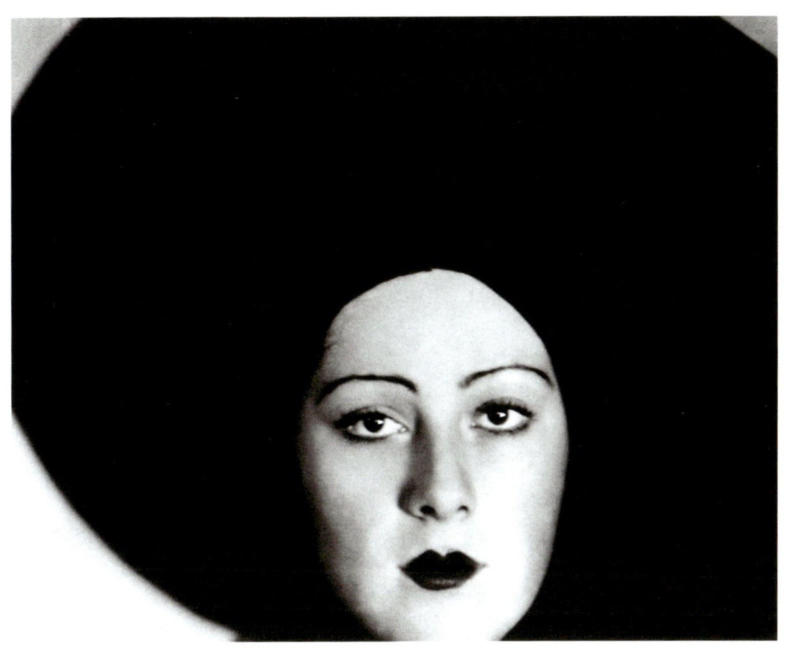

Niura Norskaya, *Dancer, Berlin, c. 1930*

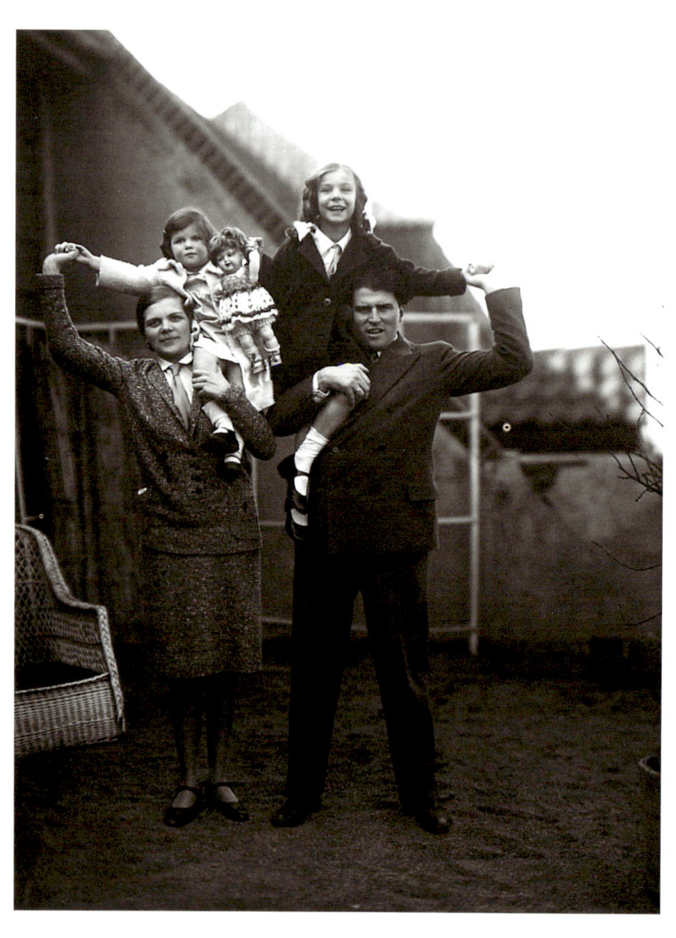

Carl Zuckmayer and family, *Berlin, c. 1929*

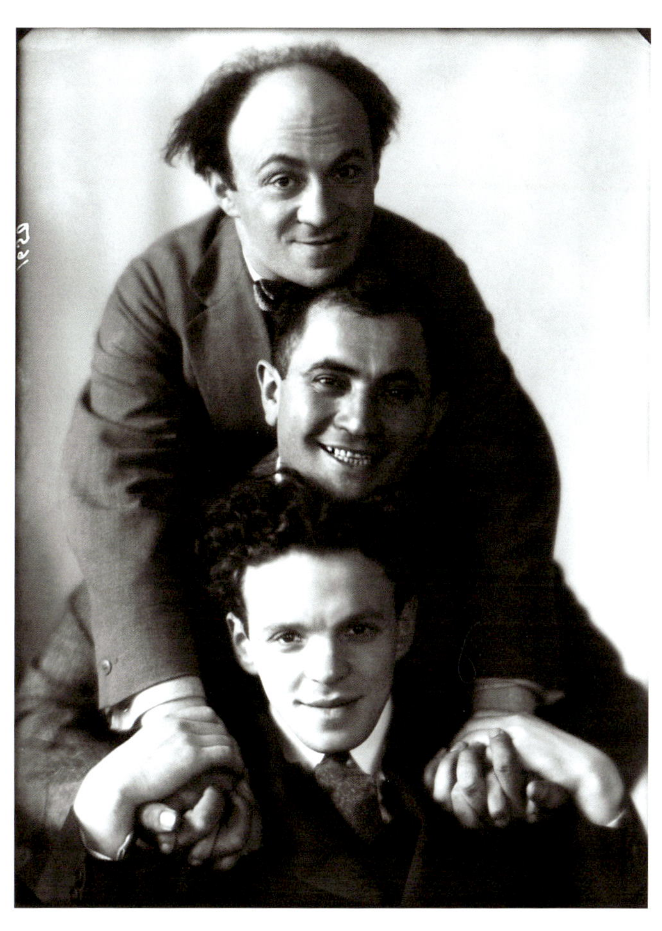

Michols, Granach, and Siskin, *Actors, Berlin, 1929*

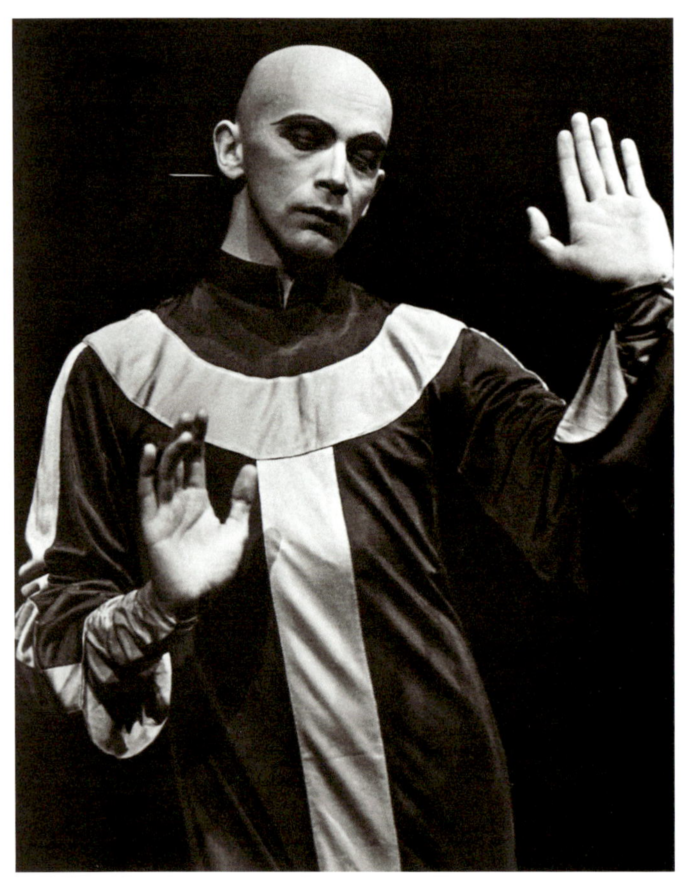

Harold Kreutzberg, *Dancer, Berlin, c. 1930*

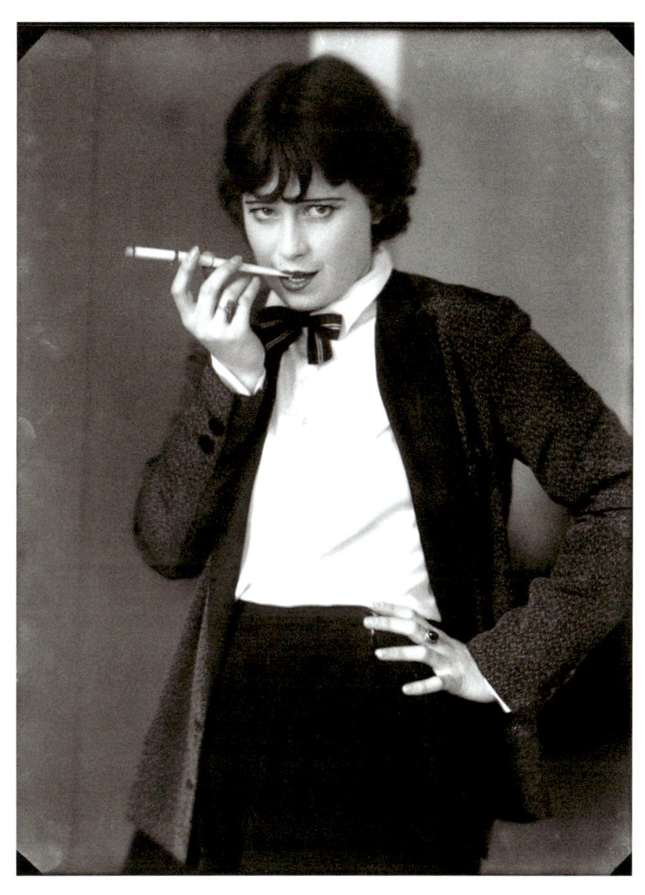

Valerie Boothby, *Actress, c. 1930*

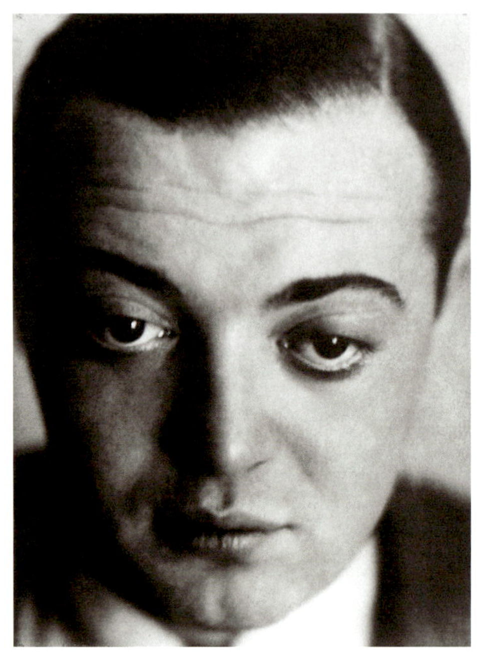

Peter Lorre, *Actor, Berlin, 1930*

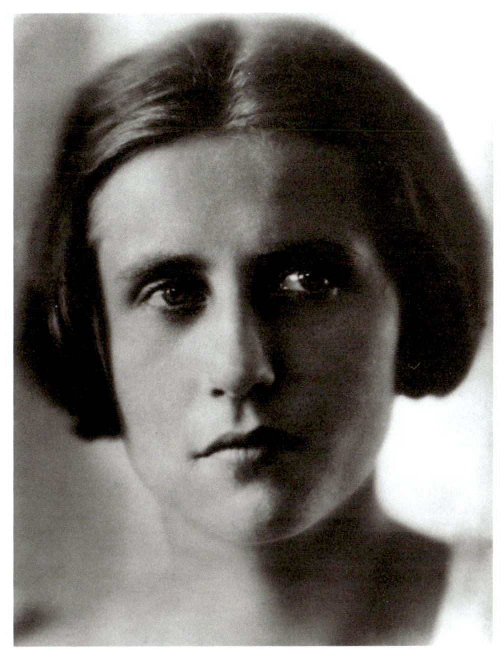

Grete Mosheim, *Actress, Berlin,* 1930

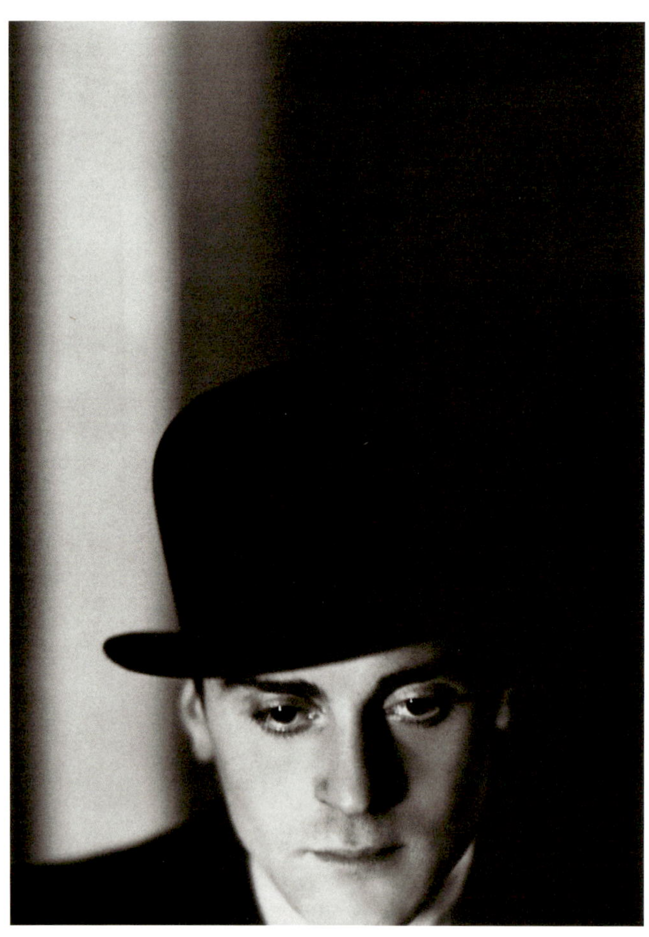

Franz Lederer, *Actor, c. 1929*

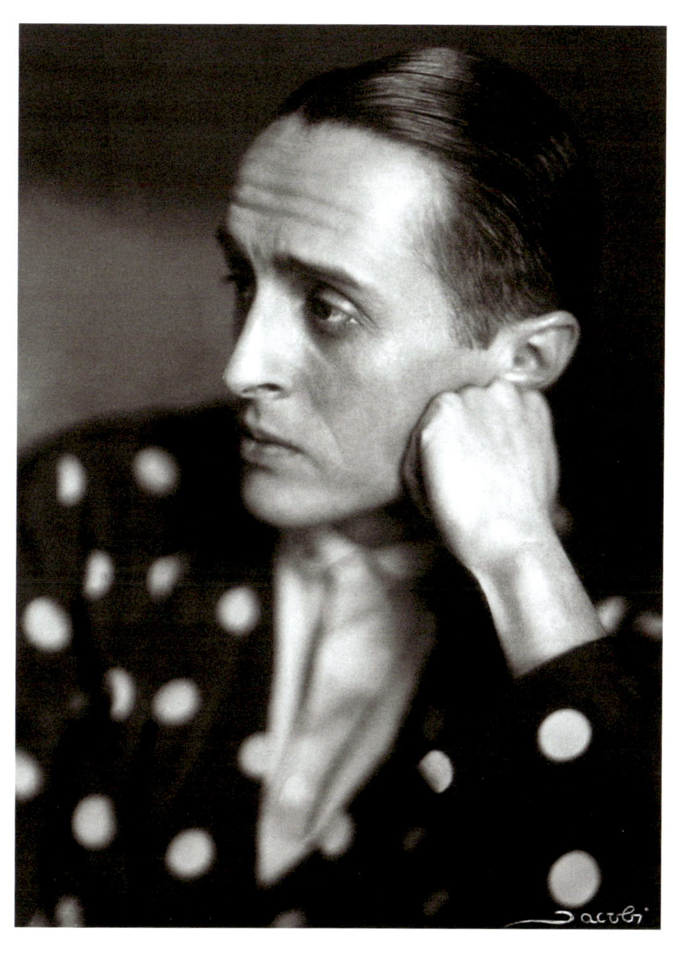

René Clair, *Director, c. 1930*

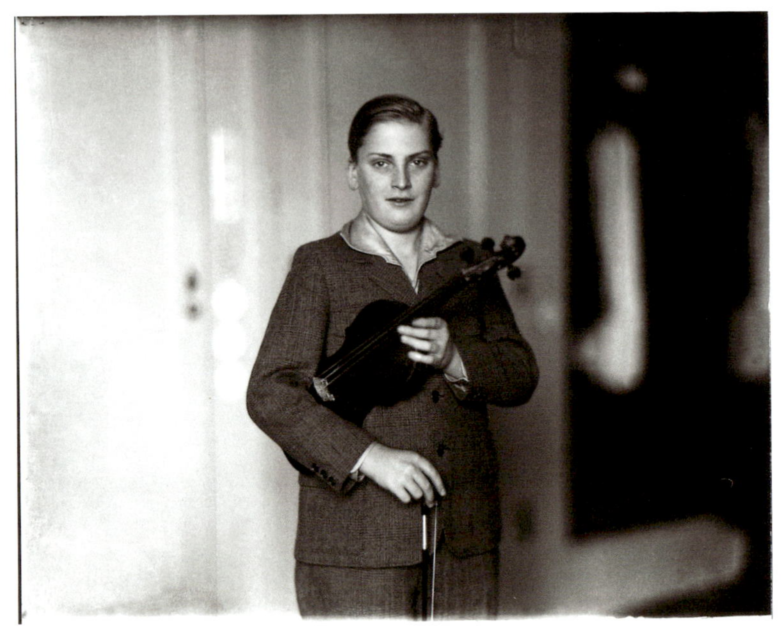

Yehudi Menuhin, *Violinist, Berlin, c. 1934*

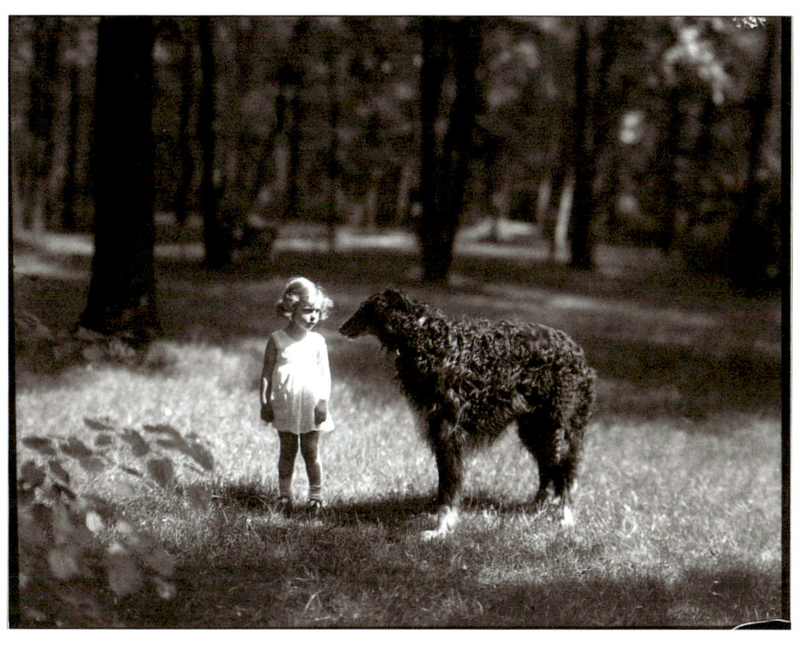

Anni Reisner, *c. 1932*

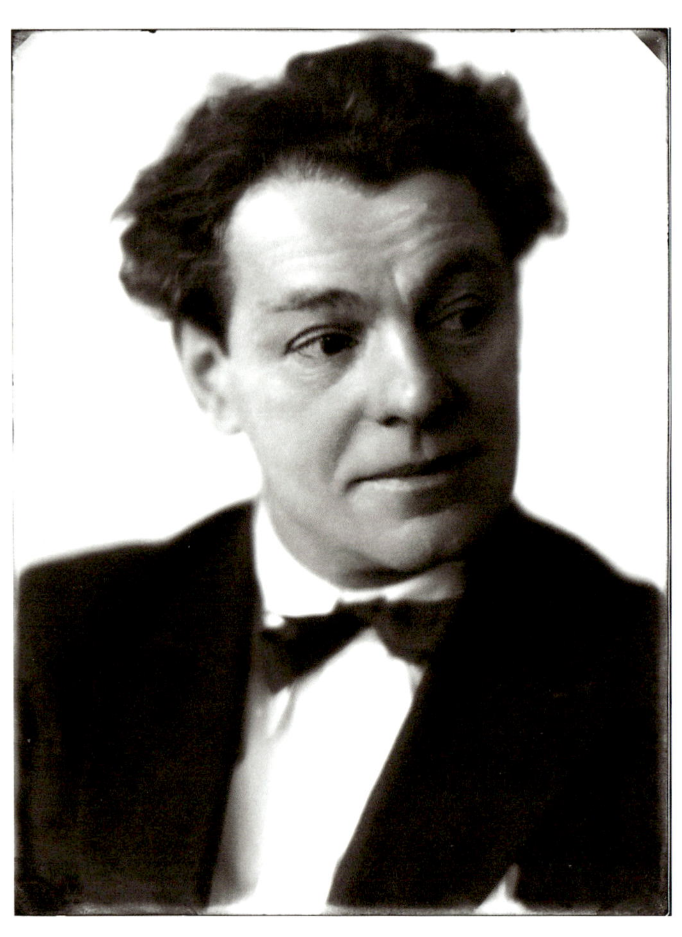

Alexander Moissi, *Actor, Berlin, 1929*

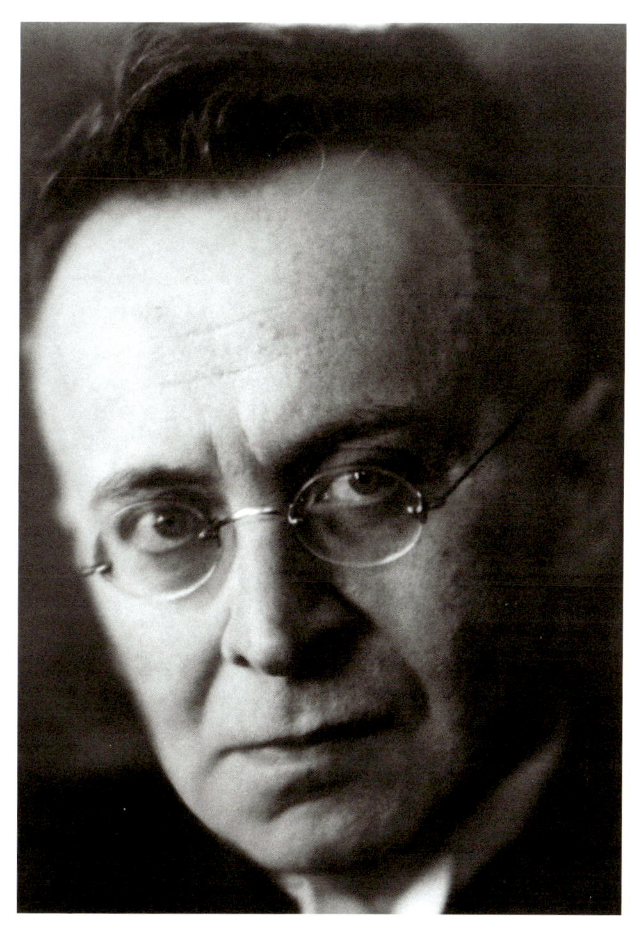

Karl Krauss, *Poet and Critic, Berlin, c. 1930*

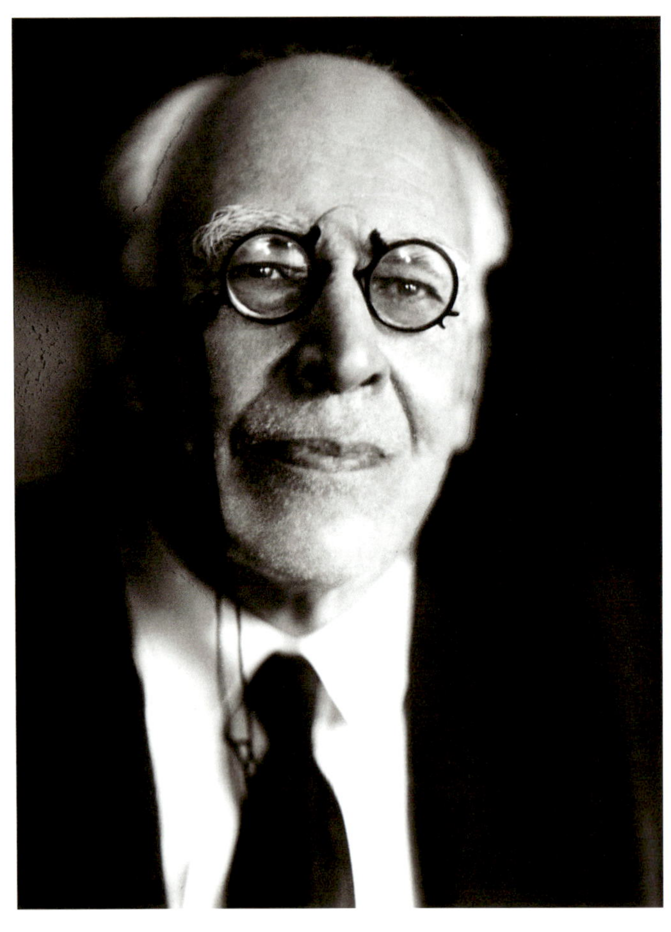

Konstantin Stanislavski, *Theater director, Berlin, 1930*

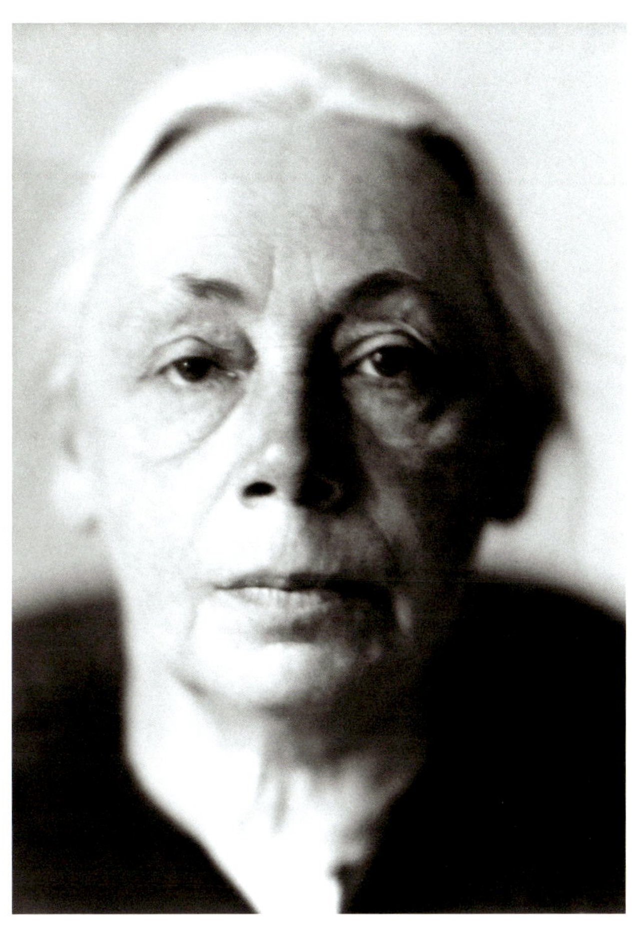

Käthe Kollwitz, *Painter and Sculptor, Berlin, 1929*

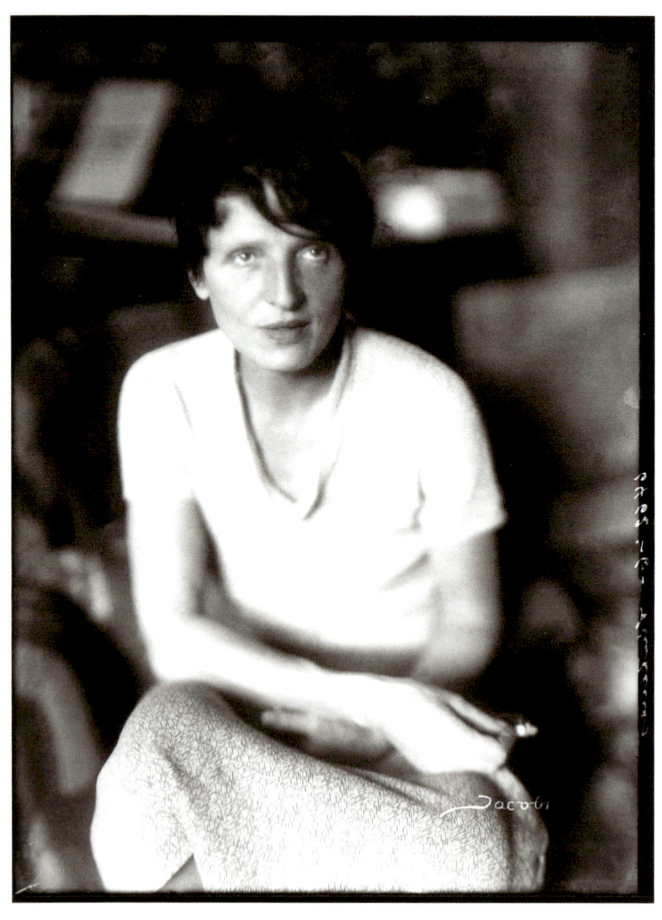

Renée Sintenis, *Sculptor, Berlin, c. 1930*

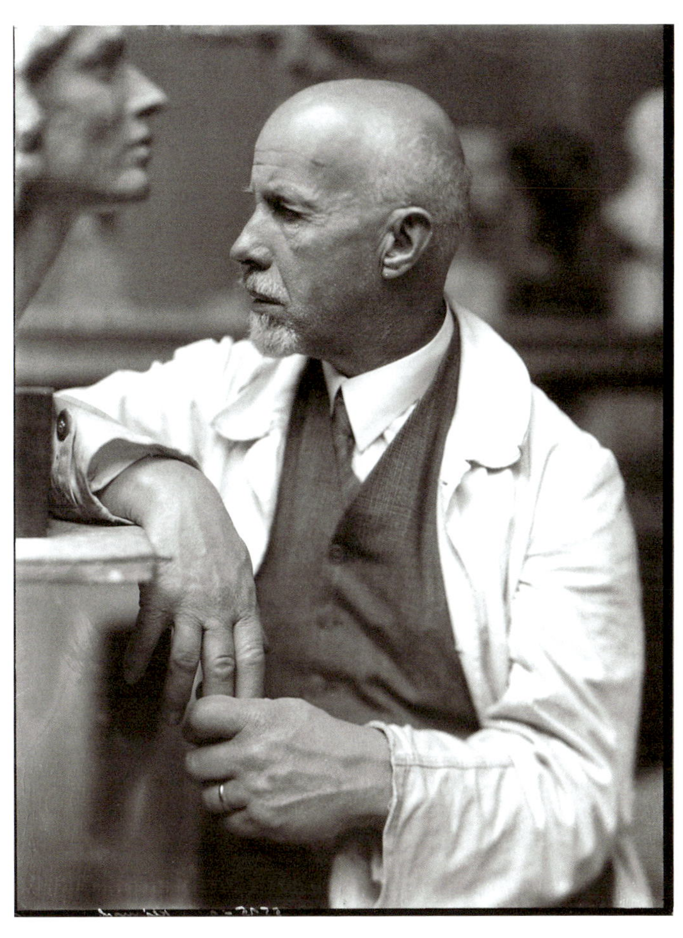

Fritz Klimsch, *Sculptor, Berlin, c. 1930*

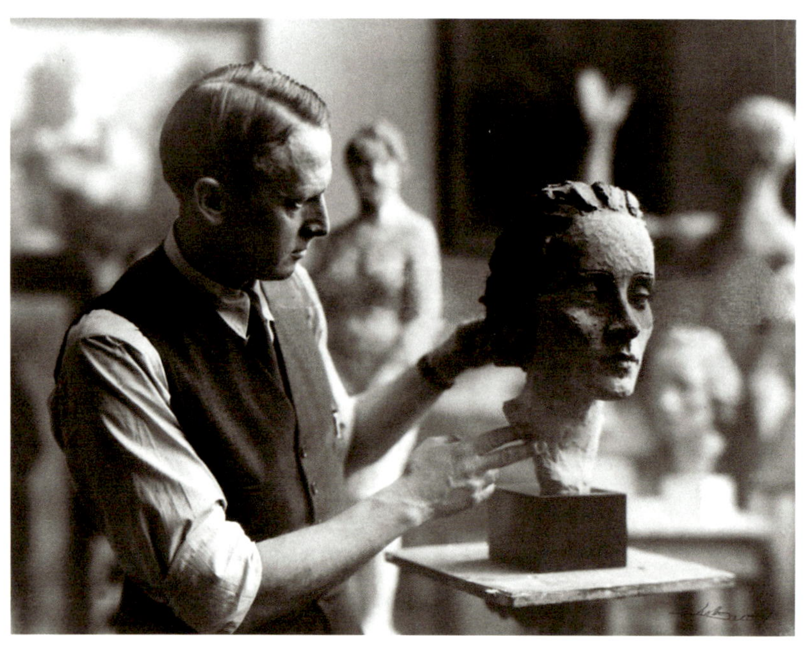

Ernesto de Fiori, *Sculptor, with a bust of Marlene Dietrich,*
Berlin, c. 1930

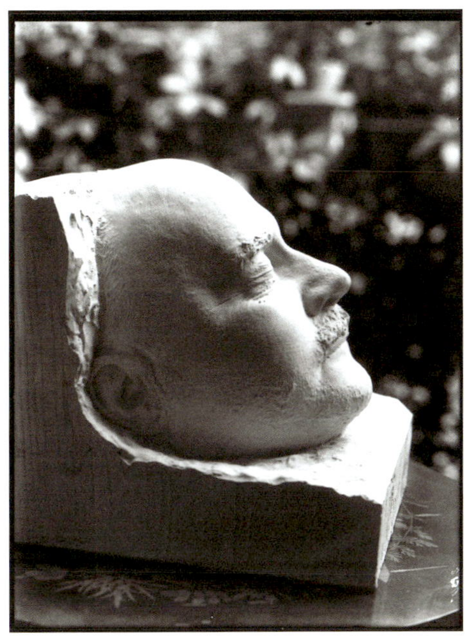

Death Mask of Dr. Blass, *Berlin*, 1930

Lotte Jacobi in her studio, *New York, 1955*
photograph by Frank H. Bauer

T N Y Y
THE NEW YORK YEARS

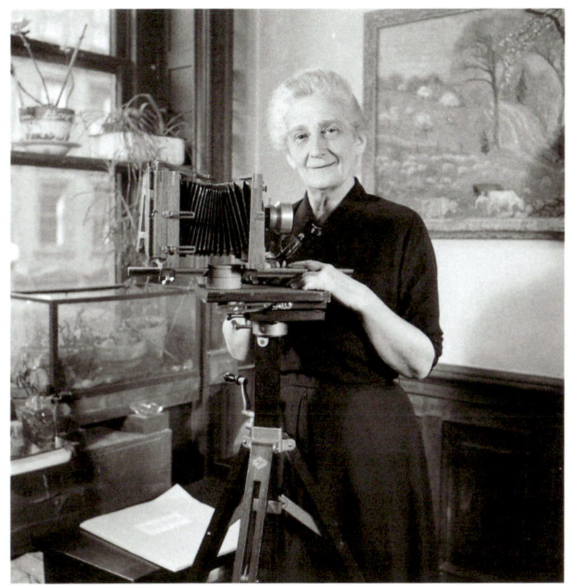

In 1935, after a brief stay in London, Lotte immigrated to New York. She met her sister Ruth, who had already established herself in America. Her mother and son arrived in February, 1936. She had to work hard to make a living and found herself photographing babies alongside distinguished European émigrés. In Berlin Jacobi had been spoiled by her large studio staff; now she worked alone, hating the drudgery of printing, and would listen to *The Shadow* or soap operas to relieve the boredom of the darkroom.[14]

She visited Alfred Stieglitz at his last gallery, An American Place, at 509 Madison Avenue. Jacobi recalled this time in her life, "At first I went to him often, but then I got busy, needed a job, met Erich Reiss, and married."[15]

Jacobi remained dedicated to Stieglitz and to his central role in modernizing American culture. To a comment challenging his prominence in the history of photography she replied, "That doesn't tell us anything about Stieglitz. It only says something about the people."[16] Lotte was tenacious in her views about the world and in her defense of friends and colleagues.

In 1940 she married Erich Reiss, a Jewish publisher whose Berlin firm, Erich Reiss Verlag (1908–1936), had been the first in Germany to publish the works of (among others) Waldo Frank, Louis Bromfield, Rose Macaulay, Thomas Masaryk, Georg Brandes, Hugo von Hofmannsthal, Maximilian Harden,

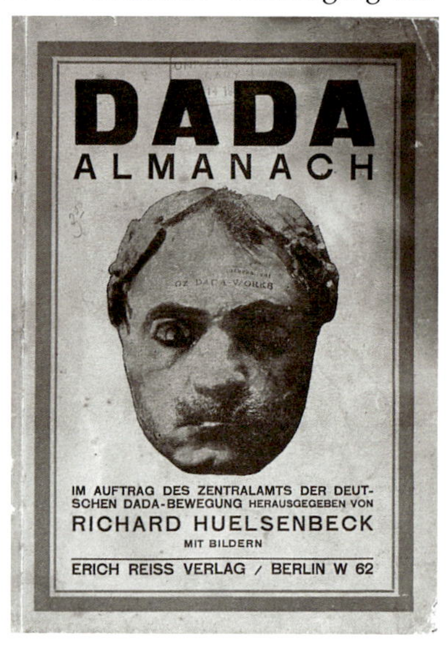

Cover of the Dada Almanach, *published by Erich Reiss Verlag in 1929*

Maeterlinck and Swift. They produced the *Dada Almanach* (1920) and *Die Sanfte: Novelle* (1920) by Dostoevsky with ten lithographs by Bruno Krauskopf.

Because of his devotion to expressionist literature and he was a Jew, Reiss was sent to a death camp and his company destroyed. He was rescued through the efforts of the Danish writer, Karin Michaelis, who engaged the help of the Scandinavian royal families. Reiss escaped to Sweden, and finally emigrated to New York.[17] He had been severely weakened by his time in the camp, and a doctor suggested he find a relaxing new hobby. Perhaps he should study photography. Lotte and Erich decided to study with Leo Katz. The two students could not have been farther removed from one another in their respective needs for a teacher; Lotte was an established artist while Erich was recovering from his many losses. Despite this disjunction, Katz — a contemplative person, who believed in the spiritual aspect of the creative process — became a teacher in life for Lotte.

Ironically, what had been prescribed as a holistic cure for Erich became a wellspring for Lotte. Katz influenced Lotte by introducing her to photogenic drawing. He encouraged her light abstractions — created without a negative by exposing photographic paper directly, with a penlight — as an inventive and fluid counterpoint to her portraits.

Katz's approach can be seen in his intervention in the career of Edward Weston. At the opening of Weston's retrospective at the Museum of Modern Art on February 12, 1946, Weston was depressed and dissatisfied with the quality of his prints. Lotte and Leo were at the reception, and Leo reminded Weston that there was more to photography and to life than a perfect procession of fine prints. This perspective helped Weston to regain his equilibrium.[18]

The photographic historian Beaumont Newhall suggested that her portraits were not sharp and the abstractions were not photo-

45

graphs, but later softened his position and wrote an introduction to an exhibition catalogue, *Light Abstractions* (1980), that reproduced the work of Coburn, Moholy-Nagy, Ray, Morgan, Kepes, Lerner, Jacobi, Sommer, Bruguière, and Corpron.

Jacobi's 1938 portrait of Albert Einstein in his study in Princeton, New Jersey, reveals a man who had already been recognized as the archetypal scientific genius. Jacobi asked him to invite his colleague, Leopold Infeld, to the session to engage her sitter in conversation while she photographed.[19] Infeld's own importance in the history of physics is confirmed by inclusion of his name in the Einstein-Infeld Theory of Relativity.

Lotte had known Einstein in Germany and had photographed him at his family home in Caputh, Germany, 1928. After his emigration to the United States she photographed him both in Princeton and sailing near his new home in Huntington, New York. In 1939 Einstein wrote to President Franklin Delano Roosevelt and warned him that German scientists might be capable of applying his theoretical knowledge to the creation of a bomb with a new level of destructive force. After the atomic bomb was used on the Japanese city of Hiroshima on August 6, 1945, killing more than sixty thousand people, Jacobi called and asked to photograph him again. He replied, "Oh Miss Jacobi, I'm an old sick man and don't want to be photographed anymore." Jacobi persevered: "But others take your picture." "Sometimes I can't avoid the press photographers," he continued, "but to you I can talk openly about it. Since that atom was thrown I feel that in a way I am guilty of it, too. For what I wanted to avoid namely that I thought that the Germans would throw it on people . . . but I never thought the Americans would do that, but they did."[20]

In the 1970s the New Hampshire Clamshell Alliance for the decommission of the Seabrook Nuclear Plant used Jacobi's most famous portrait of Einstein on a fundraising poster with her endorsement. In honor of the one-hundredth anniversary of his birth, March 14, 1979, Jacobi issued an Einstein Portfolio with twenty-five duotone reproductions printed by Thomas Todd and with an essay by Richard M. Bacon.

Lotte maintained her studio in New York from 1935 to 1955, where she also exhibited the work of such artists as Louise Nevelson, Gustav Wolf, and Stanley Hayter's Atelier 17. She remained married to Erich Reiss from 1940 until his death in 1951. The German government later paid her restitution not only for the destruction of the Jacobi archive in Berlin, but also for the demolition of Erich Reiss Verlag during the Second World War.

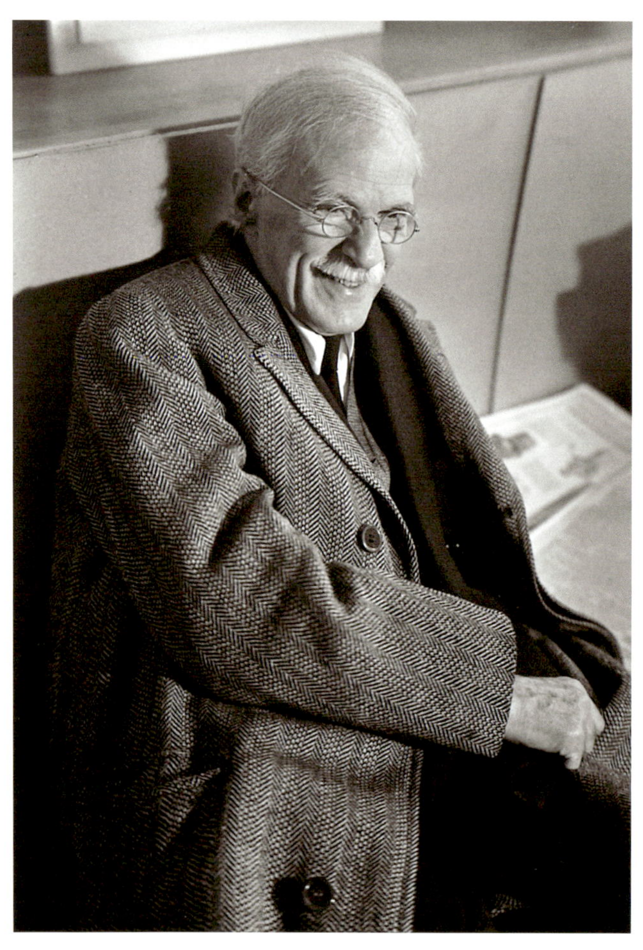

Alfred Stieglitz, *Photographer, New York, 1938*

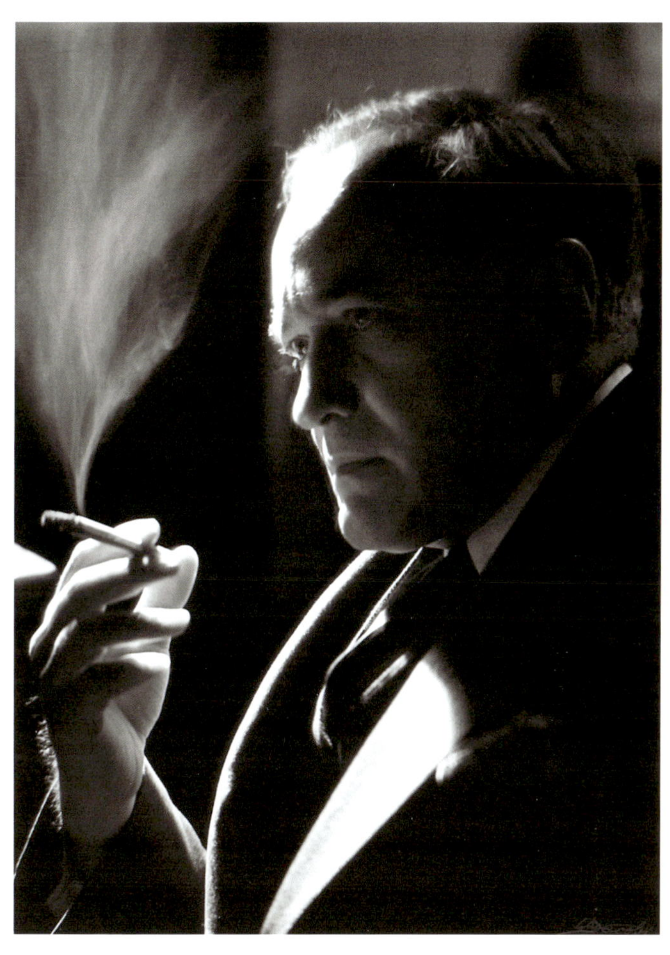

Leo Katz, *Painter, New York, 1938*

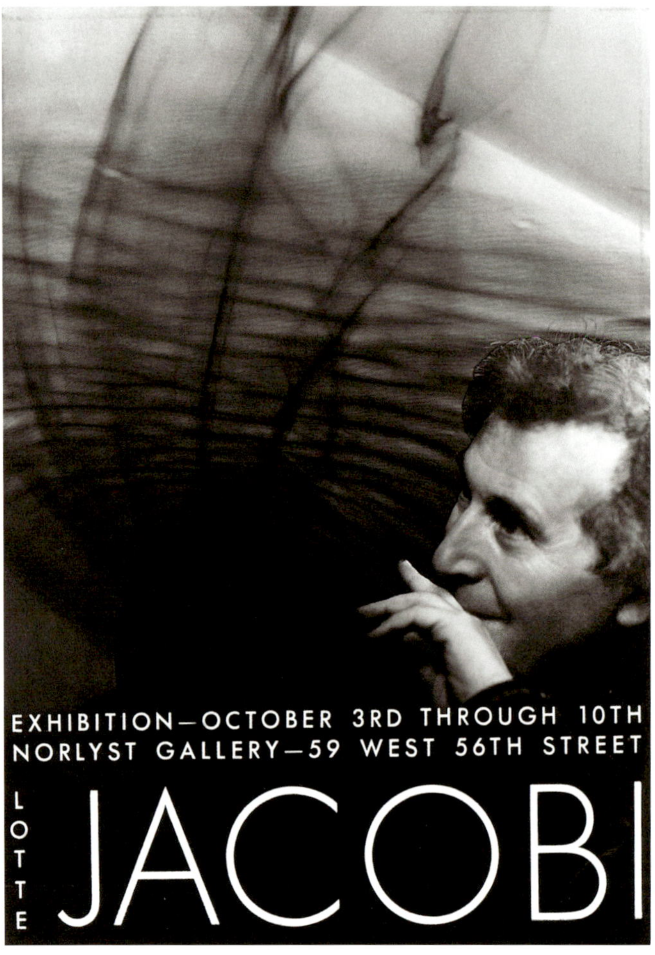

Chagall with photogenic drawing *(Norlyst Gallery announcement)*
New York, 1948

pages 51–52: *Introductory wall text by Leo Katz from the same show*

An Introduction
to the Exhibit of Lotte Jacobi

There can be little doubt that the gap between the limitations of the lens camera and the creative freedom of other graphic arts is a real one. Although many agree that it is the "Man Behind the Camera" that counts, that man can usually only "select" the section of what is before the lens. Therefore, almost all leading photo-pioneers needed contact with other arts. From Daguerre to Steichen we find leaders who were painters to begin with. Stieglitz kept an intimate, active contact with modern painting as a necessity of his life.

The introduction of Non-Objective photography changes the situation. Instead of a brush one handles a light source, and instead of the camera one uses a photosensitive surface. *Thus the procedure is no longer selective but inventive.* It offers the exhilaration of free adventure and can be as creative and bold as any other technique.

The name "Photography" (light drawing) was introduced in 1839 and has since become completely identified with camera work. "Photograms" are prints produced without a camera but with the help of objects. Completely free creations without camera and object I call "Photogenics". This is a reintroduction of a name which existed long before the term "Photography". "Photogenic Drawing and Photogenic Experiments" were known before the camera was used and before Hypo-Fixing was invented.

Today, Modern Art presents new worlds of vision, new concepts of form, space, and dimensional dynamics. Topical forces of a point, a line, a plane, and other dimensional elements are no longer static affairs to us. Composition is adjusting itself to the new dynamic Space-Energy concepts of the Atomic Era.

It was the impact of photography, among other things, which started a frantic search for "NON-OBJECTIVE" creation. Many artists gradually fled from the world of material objects to explore the forgotten realms of the subconscious mind and its symbolism. Others discovered the vast language of form-elements in space and their laws. Modern Art was shocked out of its objective, descriptive complacency, and now one finds the beginning of a return of the fruits of its labor to photography. The fact that Lotte Jacobi, a master of descriptive photography (portrait and documentary), after success and recognition in two continents finds liberation and rejuvenation in these modern worlds of visual creation, seems like the beginning of the paying of an old debt.

LEO KATZ
Chairman, Art Department
Hampton Institute

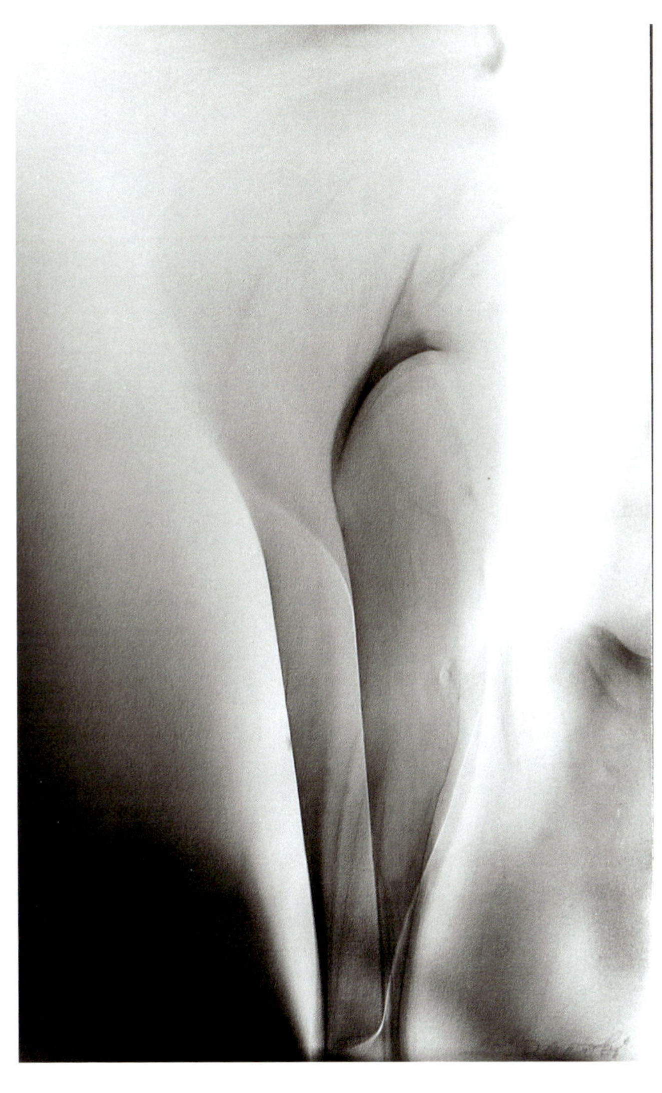

Photogenic Drawing, *c. 1946–1955*

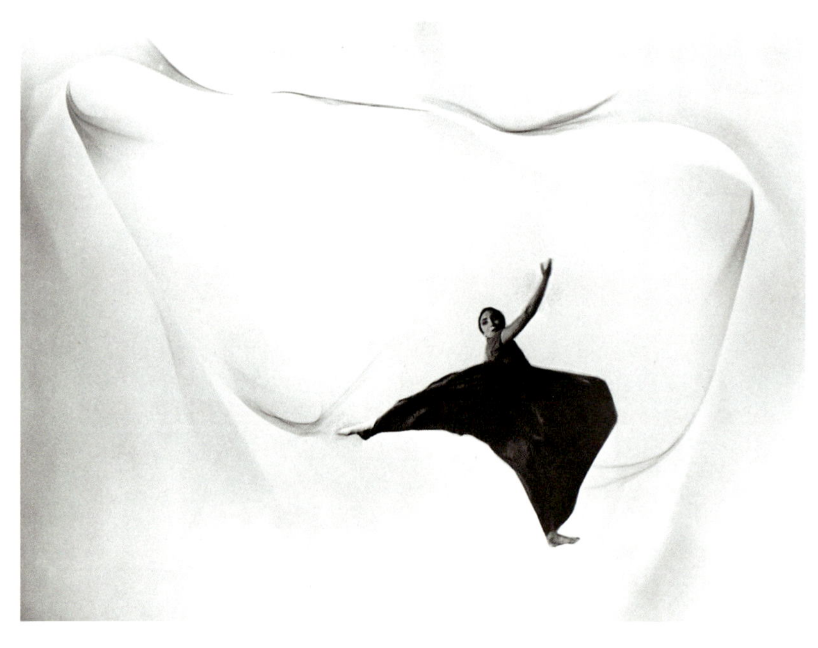

Pauline Koner with abstraction, *New York, 1939*

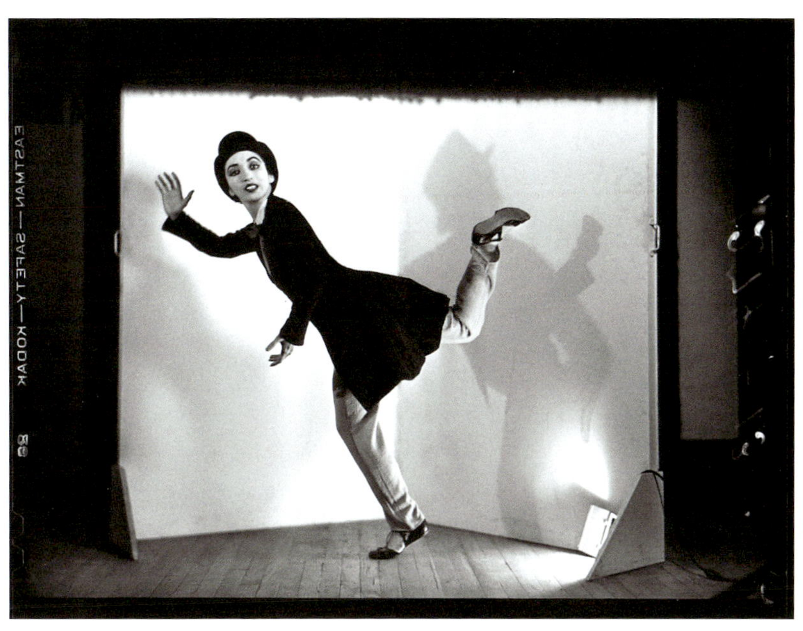

Pauline Koner, *Dancer, New York, 1939*

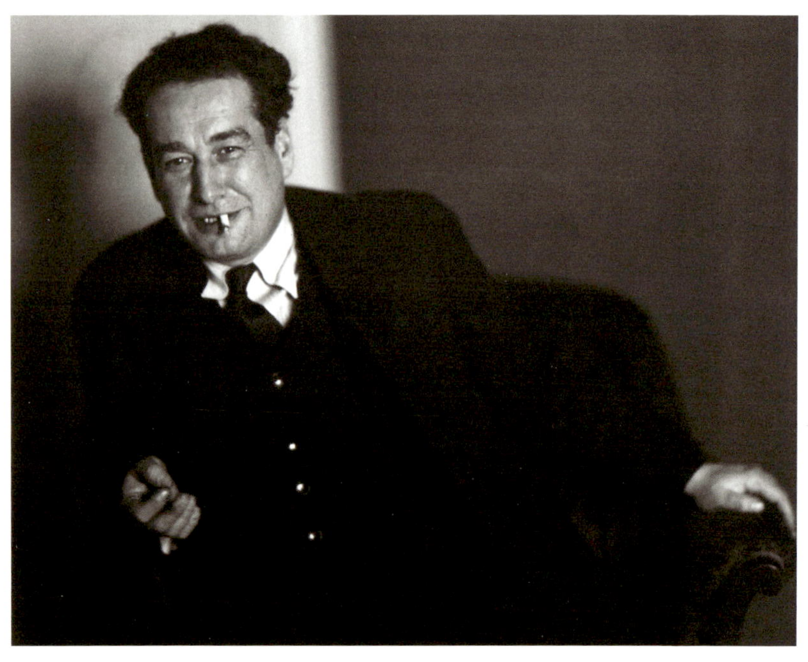

Egon Erwin Kisch, *Journalist, New York, 1940*

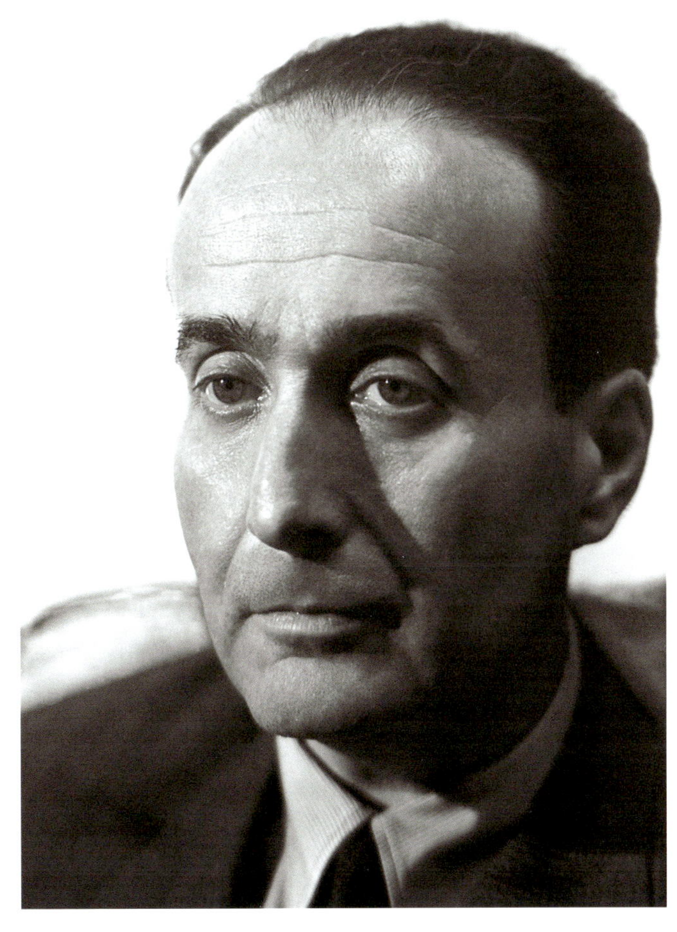

Erich Reiss, *Publisher, New York, 1940*

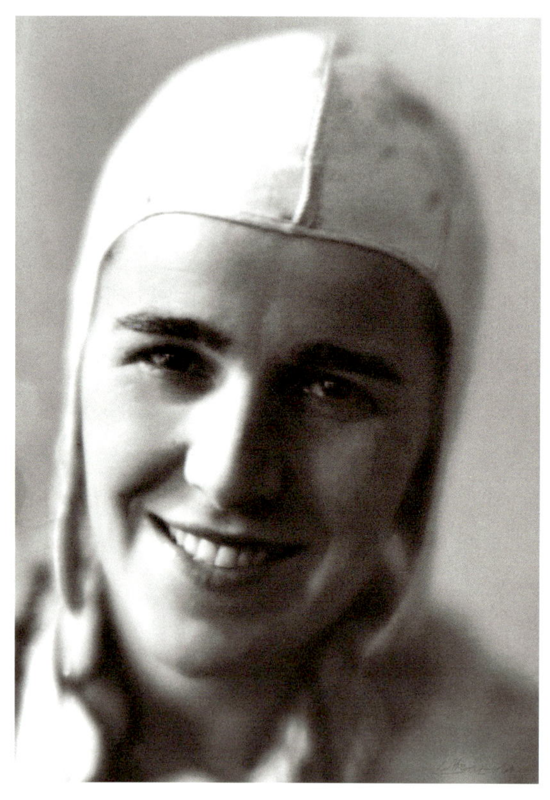

Antonie Strassmann, *Aviator*, New York, c. 1935

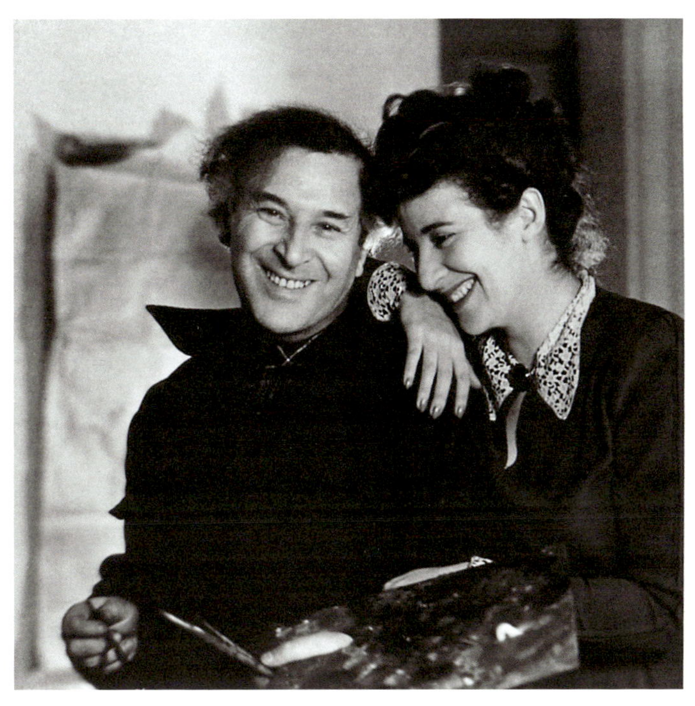

Marc Chagall and his daughter, Ida, *New York, 1945*

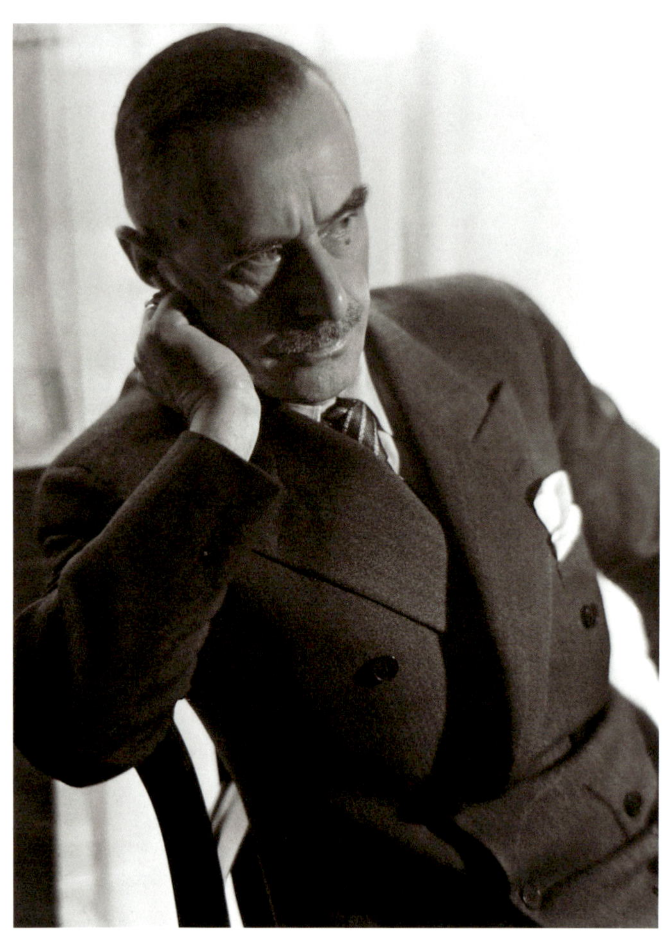

Thomas Mann, *Writer, Princeton, N.J. 1936*

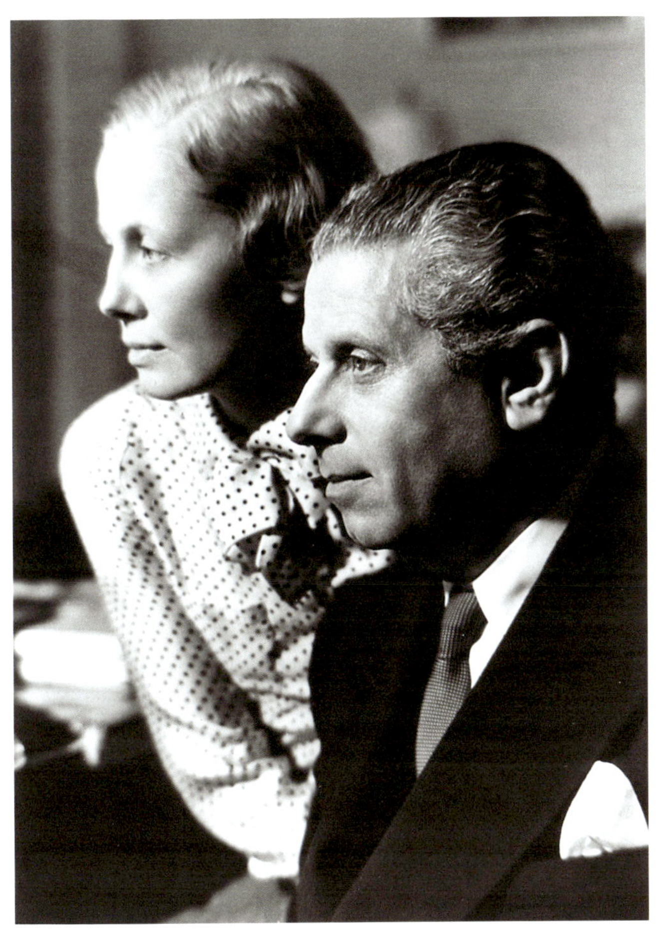

Max Reinhardt, *Actor, Director, and Producer, and his wife*, Helen Thimig, *Actress, New York, 1936*

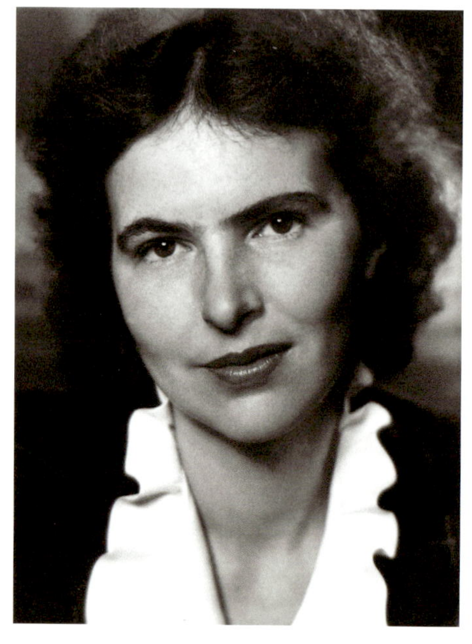

Nancy Newhall, *Writer, New York*, 1943

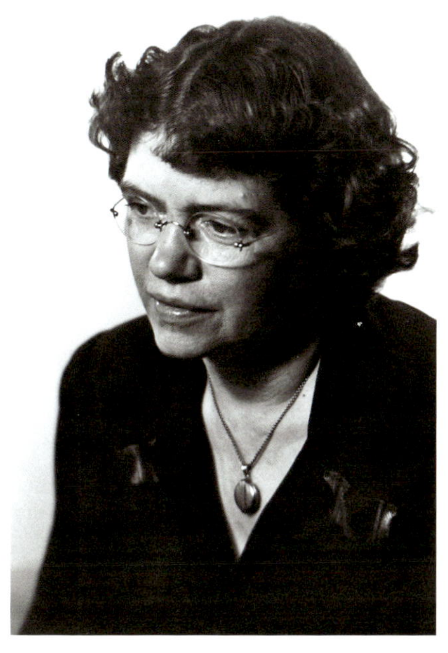

Margaret Mead, *Anthropologist, New York, 1948*

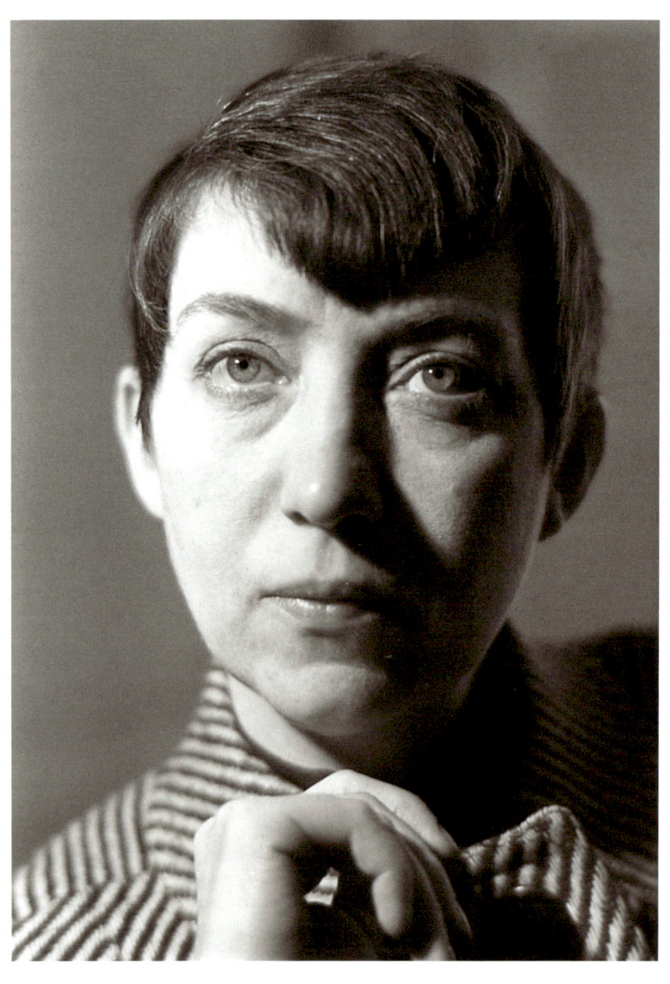

Berenice Abbott, *Photographer, New York, 1943*

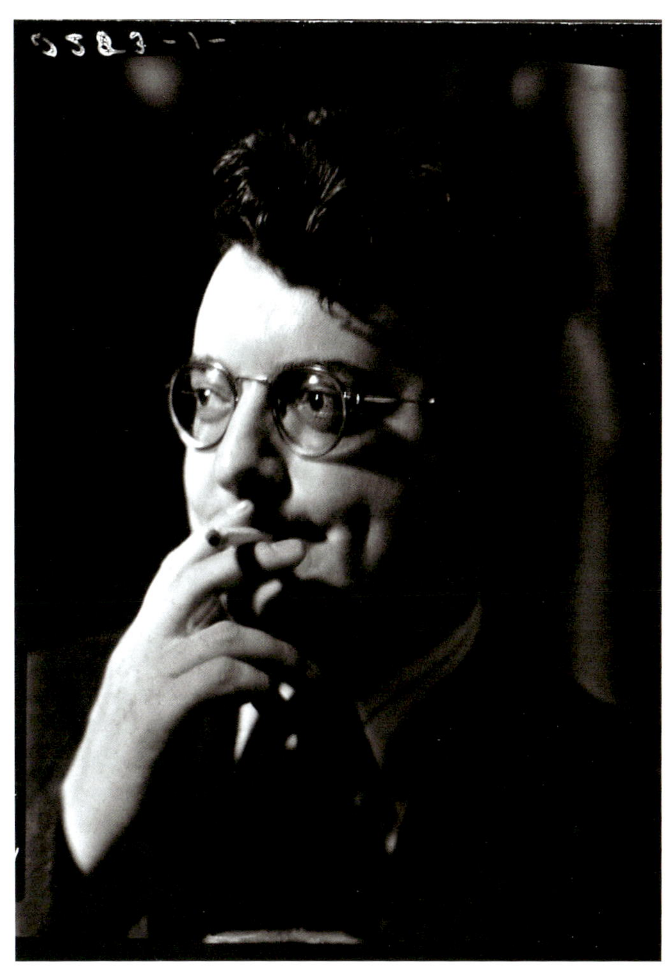

I. F. Stone, *Writer, 1936*

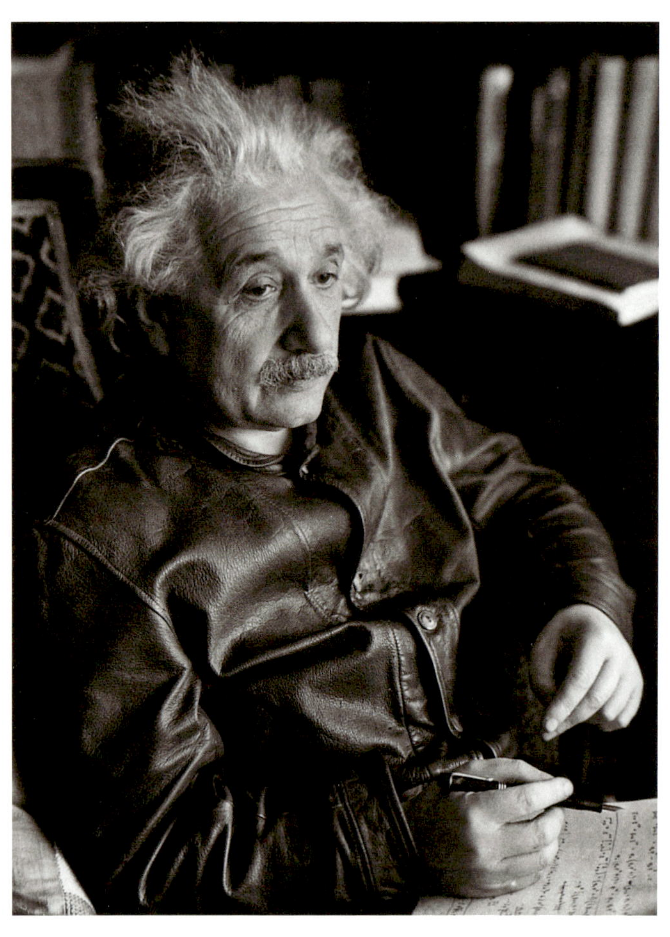

Albert Einstein, *Physicist, Princeton, N.J. 1938*

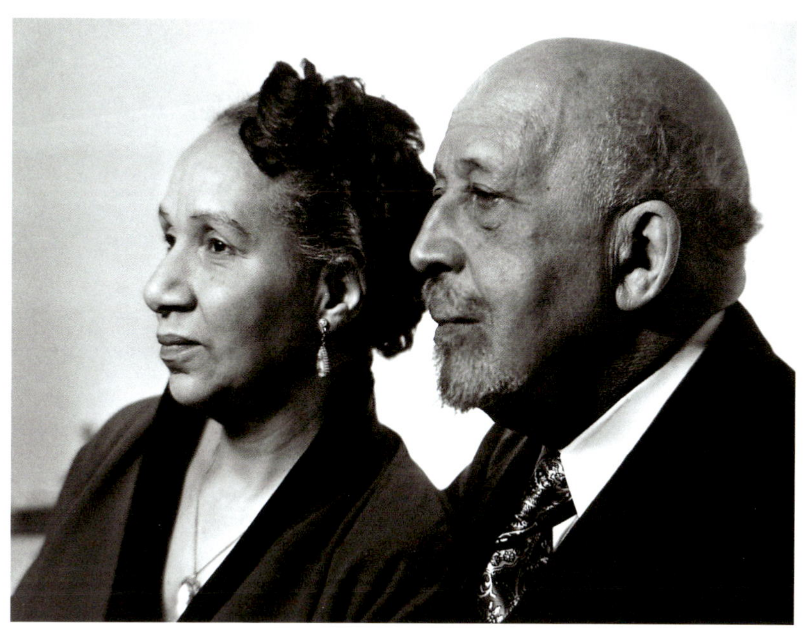

W. E. B. Du Bois, *Writer, and his wife*, Shirley Graham, *New York, c. 1950*

Lotte's study at Jacobi Place, *1976*
photograph by Peter Moriarty

Jacobi Place

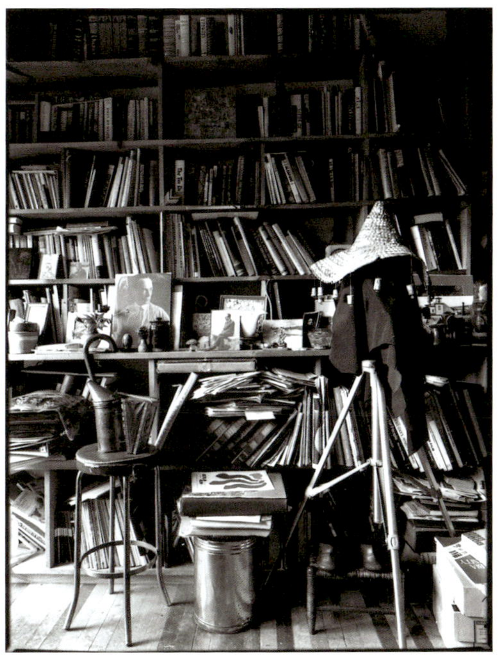

In 1955 Lotte moved to New Hampshire, initially living there with her son, John and his first wife, Beatrice Trum Hunter. She purchased a former hunting camp, gradually added to it and referred to it as "Jacobi Place." Beatrice influenced Lotte as they strove to grow vegetables in a chemical-free environment. Lotte admired both Helen and Scott Nearing in their quest to live the good life. They made a passionate effort to consider the entire ecosystem, to be responsible to all of humanity through their life's work.

In 1959 Holt Publishers commissioned Lotte to photograph the poet Robert Frost in Ripton, Vermont. Beatrice drove her the considerable distance from Deering to Ripton, but when they arrived Frost's secretary, Mrs. Morrison, told Lotte that she would be limited to only fifteen minutes to take the portrait. Lotte pho-

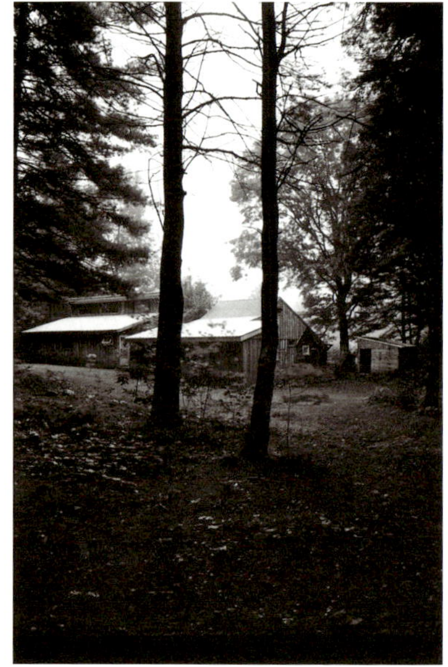

Jacobi Place, *Deering, New Hampshire, 1975*
photograph by Peter Moriarty

tographed and looked at her watch. Beatrice talked to the poet about an apple orchard in New Hampshire, that used no chemicals and about baking whole-grain bread. At the end of fifteen minutes Lotte said, "Thank you very much, Mr. Frost. Fifteen minutes is up." Frost was confused by this comment and Lotte explained the limitations imposed. He said, "Nonsense! Let's go to my studio and have a ginger beer!"[21]

In 1962 while Jacobi was far from home studying etching with Stanley Hayter in Paris, May Sarton wrote to her, "One feels divided from one's house like a snail from its shell sometimes! But it *will* wait."[22] There are two portraits of Sarton spanning the fifteen years (1955–1970) of their friendship. The photographs are reflections of Sarton's writing, which embraces the process of growing old. The correspondence between Jacobi and Sarton is moving and amorous. Lotte's life was full of kohlrabi and pure honey, but it lacked adult love. Sarton sent her Valentines, and, in *At Seventy: A Journal,* wrote, "Lotte in her old age has become an astonishing beauty. She so obviously enjoys being herself, being the center of a great deal of attention, being the wise one and the mischievous one, too, for she is a great tease. . . ."[23]

During the 1960s Lotte's bohemian nature and her past experience with the cabarets of Berlin suddenly came in confluence with the American Revolution. She became a mentor to young people — some of them photographers. Minor White visited Jacobi Place and she exhibited his photographs in her studio. White reciprocated his admiration for her work by including it in *Light 7,* an exhibition and catalogue, which reflected their mutual belief in the central role of the spiritual in art. When they exchanged prints Lotte chose *Easter Sunday* (1963), which responds to light on water in a way that is akin to her use of the penlight on paper in her photogenic drawings.

In addition to White's work, Jacobi exhibited the work of other prominent artists. Notable examples included Robert and Frances Flaherty's still photographs from the Thunder Bay region (*c.* 1910) which anticipated the landmark film, *Nanook of the North* (1922); Albert Renger-Patzsch's prints from *Die Welt ist schön* (1928); the work of Christopher Cook; and the etchings of Leo Katz. Paul Caponigro visited her Deering studio several times and corresponded with her for more than a decade. Lotte denied claims that she played the role of mentor with him; he was already an established photographer when they met. Nonetheless on August 11, 1966, he wrote to her while sailing to Ireland to photograph megalithic stones: "Eleanor and I were both hoping to speak more with you about some of the subjects we touched on regarding the idea of soul. . . . We'll pick up where we left off when we get back — what I am looking for in Ireland (or anywhere) relates to this matter."[24]

One month after Lotte's death Caponigro wrote to Beatrice Trum Hunter, "Eleanor and I had such good visits with her — and sadly note there are very few 'depth-seekers' like Lotte these days."[25]

In the spring of 1973 my teacher, Richard Merritt said, "It is time for you to go to visit Lotte." At that point I didn't realize that I was following a tradition by visiting Jacobi Place. From the beginning she responded to my photographs with a profound candor. At our first meeting she silently divided my pictures into two groups. She pointed to the left-hand pile and said, "You can forget about these." She then turned her attention to the group of prints on the right and continued, "These photographs begin to say something about the people." During that summer I followed her guidance and studied with Paul Caponigro in Maine. During a break from photographing at Mosquito Point, he looked at an apple, picked it up, and cut it, saying, "How many people ever take the time to look?" His personal intensity and his photograph *Apple* (1964) were life-changing experiences for me.

DURING THE 1970s Lotte remained socially, artistically, and politically active. In 1977 she received a grant from the National Endowment for the Arts to photograph artists. She was a delegate from New Hampshire to the Democratic Convention and an Advocate for the Arts from the state of New Hampshire to Washington, D.C. After Jacobi visited President Jimmy Carter and his wife in Plains, Georgia, he wrote to her on September 14, 1982, "Rosalynn and I appreciate the wonderful photographs and the jars of honey."[26]

It was her nature to be a political activist. Our conversations were somewhat comical as I strove to document the role she and her family played in the history of photography. She'd listen, but quietly redirect our discussion with potent statements like: "The wind isn't used. The sun isn't used. The things that are on Earth and are free for the asking aren't used. And the food, what good is still left in the food is then by processing really gotten rid of, so that we only get things that aren't really healthy for us."[27]

LOTTE OUTLIVED HER SON John, who died in 1985. This unfortunate event meant that she spent her last years at a group home in Concord, New Hampshire. When I visited her, she pointed at a caged bird and said, "So there is a bird and here am I." I had made two loaves of sourdough bread and she decisively chose the rye over the wheat bread with a curious tilt of her head. She died on May 6, 1990 just three months prior to her ninety-fourth birthday. On June 16, 1990 there was a remembrance held in her honor at the University of New Hampshire. This was an appropriate site to gather friends and colleagues; she had been involved with the school in a variety of ways while she was a resident of the state. She sent botanical samples from her garden for identification by the faculty, served as a mentor to aspiring photographers, exhibited her pictures in the Paul Creative Arts Center, and established her archive in the Diamond Library. In 1974 the university awarded her an honorary degree and recognized her diverse contributions to the state. The historian Margaretta Mitchell was not able to attend the ceremony, but wrote to Beatrice Trum Hunter, "I loved her for her wit and wisdom and the honesty of her vision."[28]

Alan Fern of the National Portrait Gallery in Washington, D.C., reflected, "I am sure the recent years of inactivity must have been very difficult for her; my own picture of her recalls a perpetual motion device, or perhaps a hummingbird with remarkable metabolic rate concealed in the disguise of a fragile elderly lady with a camera in one hand."[29]

Although Lotte Jacobi's work was not included in the initial surveys of photographic history by Beaumont Newhall (1938) or Helmut and Alison Gernsheim (1955), a second generation of curators and collectors is reassessing her place in the history of this young medium as we enter the new millennium. Today her work forms part of museum collections throughout the world, and it has appeared in publications with a variety of viewpoints: feminist revisions of photographic history, German surveys of the Weimar era, American summaries of modernist work, French general histories of photography among them. Curators with a special interest in cameraless light abstraction and the Fuji Corporation in Japan have added Lotte's work to their collections.

In addition to the public holdings of her work, private collectors benefited from her practice of making original, signed photographic postcards of her work. She used these prints as an expression of friendship and was perhaps inspired by the Stieglitz use of postcard prints for his series of cloud pictures, the *Equivalents*.

In 1977 when she was eighty-one years old she called me in Rochester, New York, where I was a graduate student. She said that she and her girlfriends were traveling to the Beechwold Clinic in Ohio. They had sleeping bags, and wanted to stay at my apartment. I convinced her to take my bed while I slept on the floor. In the morning she spread out about twenty postcard prints and said, "Is there anything that you like?" At my request she signed each print. Through this practice Lotte expressed the cult value of photography, which was for Roland Barthes as important as its exhibition value.

When Lotte photographed Marc Chagall and his daughter Ida in 1945, Chagall was pleased with her work and ordered several prints from various negatives. Lotte indicated that she could not print them identically and when Chagall saw the variations he said, "Now I see that photography has the possibility of being an art."[30] While Stieglitz might have been delighted by Chagall's pronouncement as a step forward in his efforts to have photography recognized as a fine art, Jacobi was ultimately more involved in contributing to a humane world than in narrowly formal studies. When we consider her photographs, we should view them as an extension of a consciousness, formed during the experimental years of the Weimar era, that engaged people and evolved for six decades.

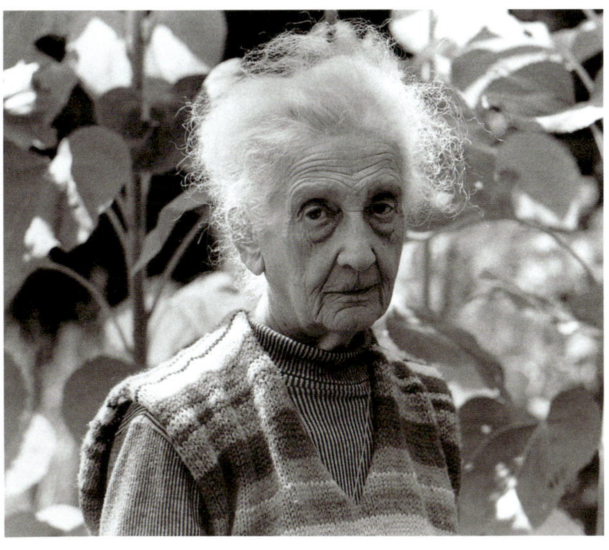

Lotte at Jacobi Place, *Deering, New Hampshire, 1975*
photograph by Peter Moriarty

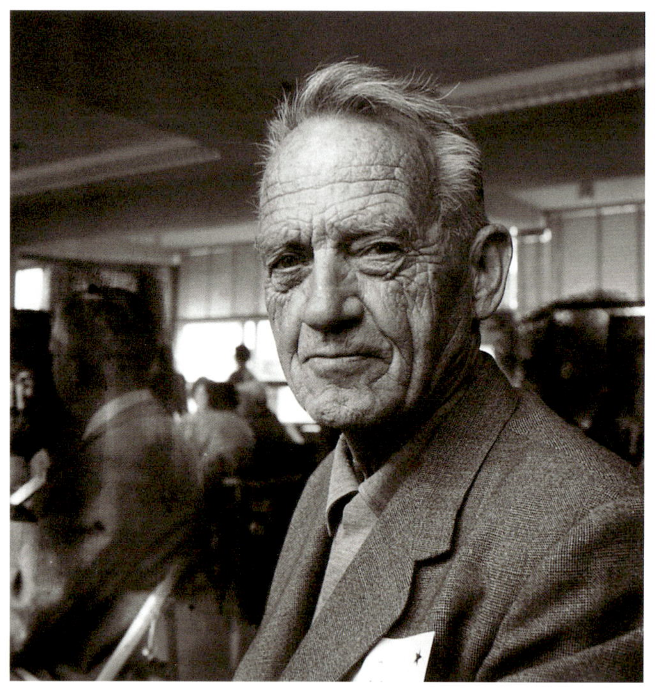

Scott Nearing, *Writer, Maine, 1973*

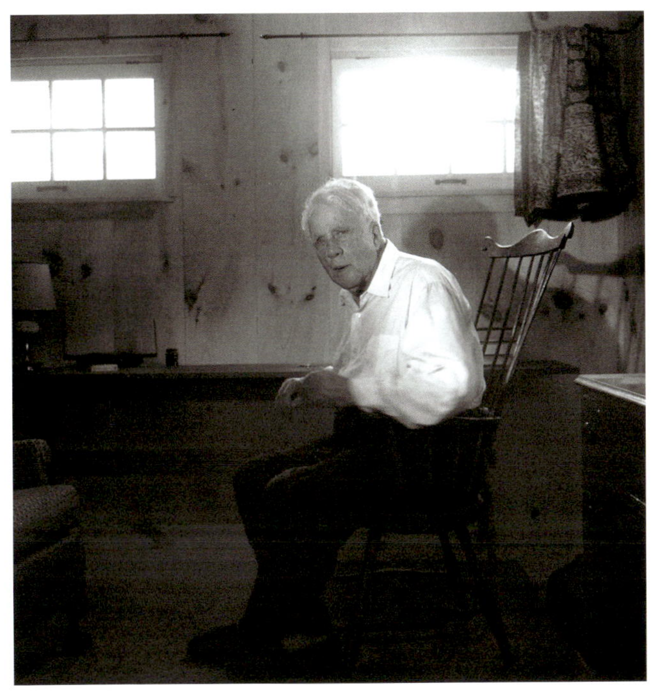

Robert Frost, *Poet, Ripton, Vermont*, 1959

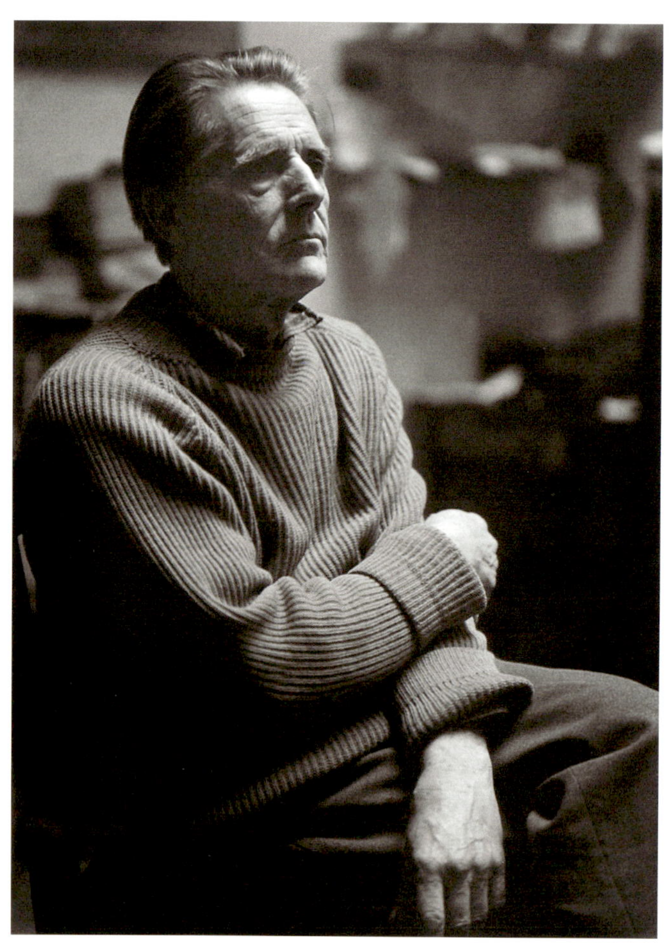

Stanley Hayter, *Painter, Paris, 1973*

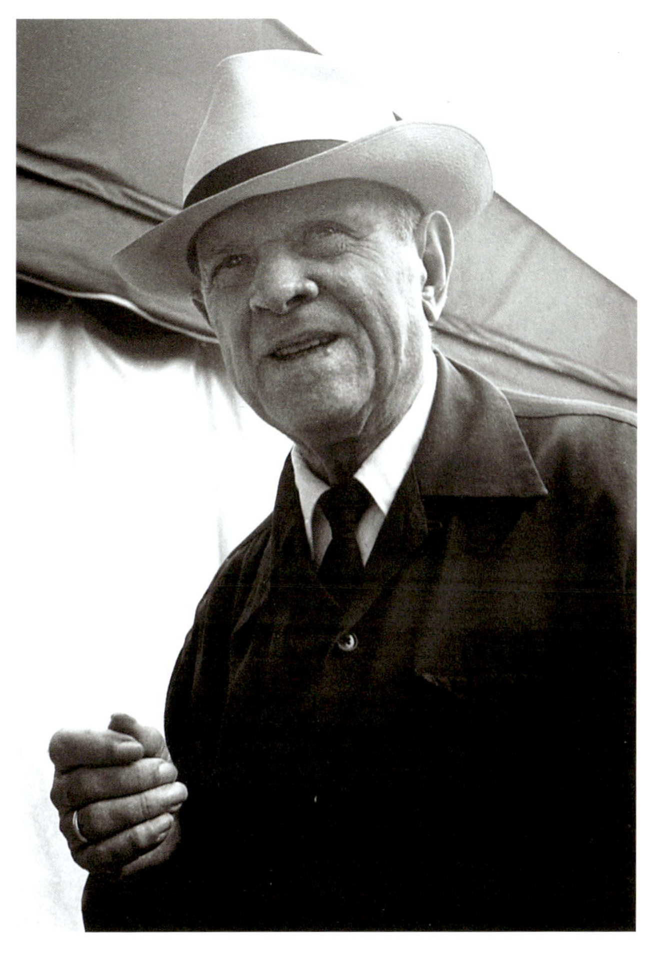

Pablo Casals, *Cellist and Conductor, Marlboro, Vermont, 1967*

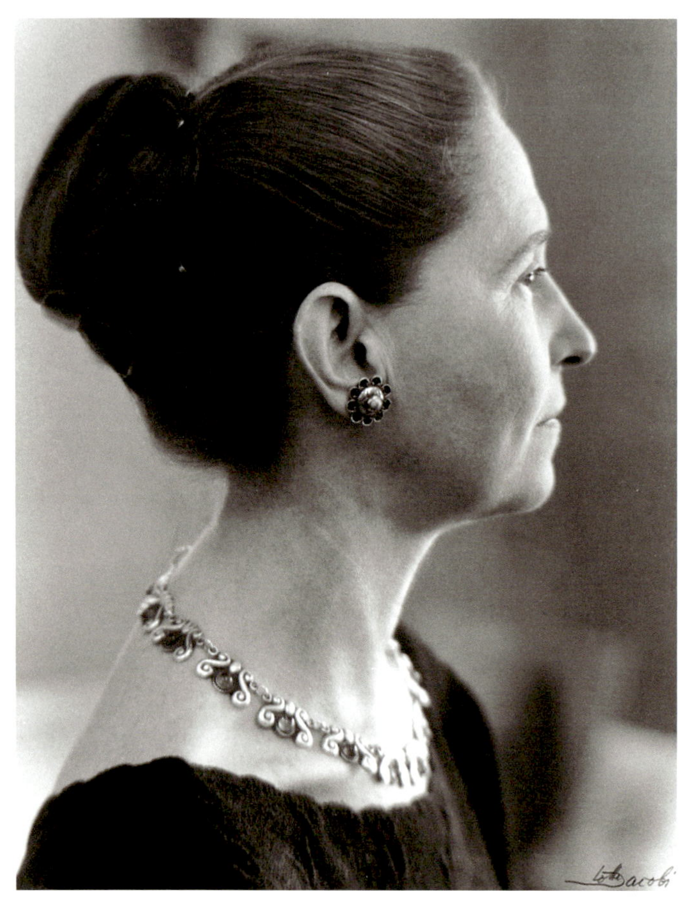

Beatrice Trum Hunter, *1971*

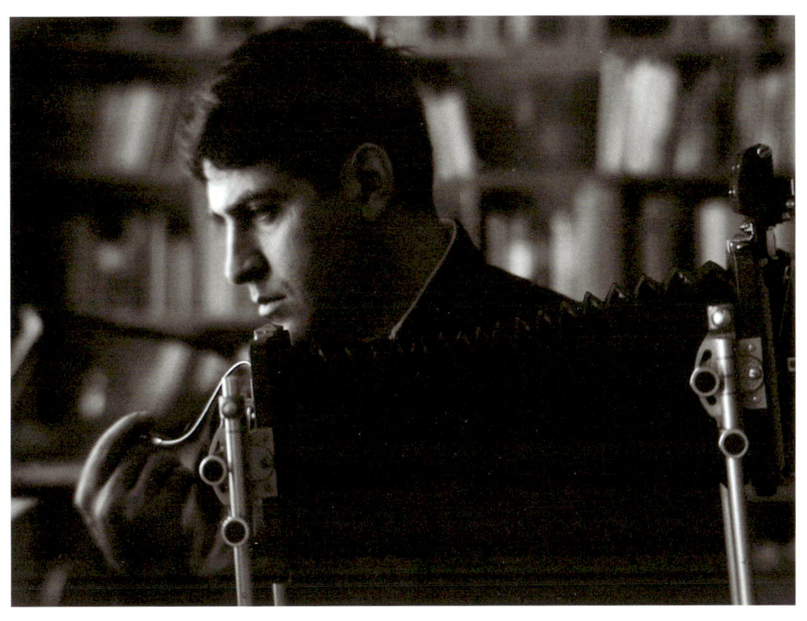

Paul Caponigro, *Photographer, Deering, New Hampshire, c. 1965*

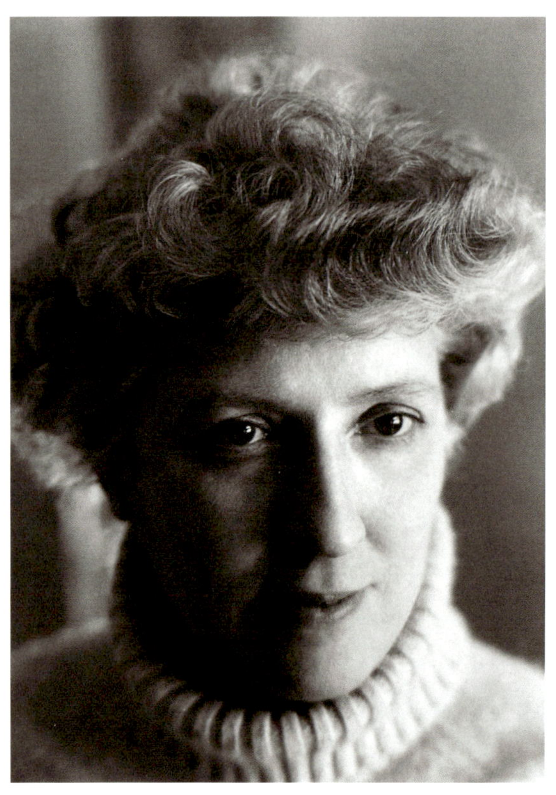

May Sarton, *Poet*, 1955

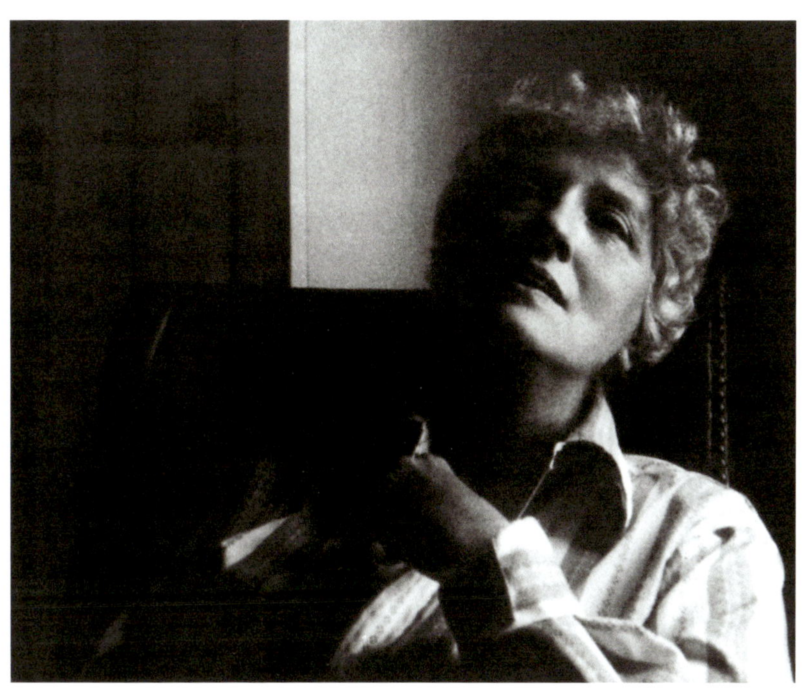

May Sarton, 1970

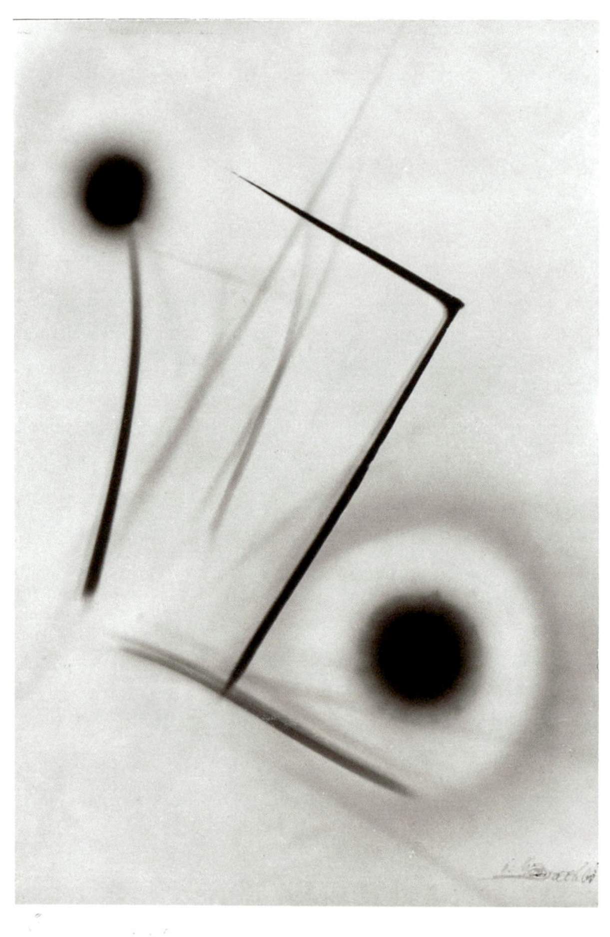

Photogenic Drawing, 1965

Lotte Jacobi's Circle

MARTIN BUBER (1878–1965) published *Ich und Du* (*I and Thou*, 1923) and later translated the Hebrew Bible into German (1926–37). He was a world-renowned philosopher, theologian, and writer.

MARC CHAGALL (1887–1985), an artist from Belarus, was exiled from the Soviet Union in 1923. He worked with Diaghilev's Ballets Russes in Paris and benefited from Ambroise Vollard's sponsorship before he came to the United States in 1941.

PAUL CAPONIGRO (B. 1932) is an American photographer who has received Guggenheim grants in support of his work and has published a number of distinguished books of photographs. He was a former music student and an assistant to Minor White.

JIMMY CARTER (B. 1924) was president of the United States from 1977–81 and received the Martin Luther King Jr. Nonviolent Peace Prize in 1979. He continues to be a leader in negotiating peace between nations and supporting free election of government officials.

RENÉ CLAIR (1891–1981) was a French filmmaker, who worked in both documentary (*Paris qui dort*, 1925), and fiction genres (*A Nous la liberté*, 1931). He is considered a central artist of the golden era of French film.

LOUIS-JACQUES MANDÉ DAGUERRE (1787–1851) was intrigued by illusion. He created two dioramas (Paris, 1822, and London, 1833) before his most famous invention, the daguerreotype, was announced in Paris on January 7, 1839. He published his *Historique et description des procédés du Daguerréotype et du Diorama* before the end of the same year.

ALBERT EINSTEIN (1879–1955) was born in Ulm, Germany. In 1905 he introduced the Special Theory of Relativity for which he was awarded the Nobel Prize for Physics. From 1933–55 he conducted research at the Institute for Advanced Study in Princeton. He published *Why War?* (1933) with Sigmund Freud.

UTE ESKILDSEN (B. 1947) was the assistant to Otto Steinert in the production of Lotte Jacobi's 1974 exhibition at the Museum Folkwang, Essen, Germany. She is currently the curator of photographs at the museum.

ROBERT FROST (1874–1963) was an American poet rooted in New England who received Pulitzer prizes (1924, 1931, 1937, and 1943) for his work. His landmark work is embedded in American culture.

BEATRICE TRUM HUNTER (B. 1918) is a writer, nutritionist and editor who is concerned about the health of our planet. She has written more than twenty books on food issues, including *Gardening Without Poisons* (1964) and is the food editor of Consumers' Research, Inc.. She was Lotte's first daughter-in-law and remains her kindred spirit.

JOHN HUNTER (1917–1985) Lotte's only child, was a rare coin dealer in Hillsboro, New Hampshire. He is survived by his second wife, Bernadette Hunter, who now lives in Paris, France.

LEOPOLD INFELD (1898–1968) was a Polish physicist who worked with Einstein at Princeton (1936–38) and published *The Evolution of Physics* (1938) with him. He later wrote a biography, *Albert Einstein* (1950).

LEO KATZ (1887–1982) was a Austrian-born painter and mentor who instructed Lotte and her husband, Erich Reiss, in photography in New York. He encouraged Lotte's abstract photogenic drawings and a spiritual approach to art. He was a board member of The Foundation for Mind Research with Alan Watts, Joseph Campbell, and Margaret Mead.

EGON ERWIN KISCH (1885–1948) was a progressive Czechoslovakian writer. Known as the Raging Reporter, he promoted reportage as a journalistic style. In 1933 he was taken to a Nazi concentration camp, but escaped. A friend of both

Lotte and Erich Reiss, he tried to introduce the two in Germany, but only suc-
ceded in doing so years later in New York City.

KÄTHE KOLLWITZ (1867–1945) was a German painter, printmaker, and sculptor. She was the first woman to hold the directorship of the Prussian Academy of
Arts, but was asked to resign (May 15, 1933) because of her liberal politics. In
1943 her Berlin home was destroyed.

PAULINE KONER (B. 1912) was a dancer who believed in intrinsic rather extrinsic movement. She founded her own company with Doris Humphrey in 1949.
She explored the close-up medium of television as it applied to dance.

LOTTE LENYA (1898–1981) was an Austrian singer and dancer who studied
dance in Zürich (1914–20) before moving to Berlin in 1920. She became
famous in the role of Jenny in Bertolt Brecht and Kurt Weill's *Die Dreigroschenoper* (1928). She was married to Kurt Weill

PETER LORRE (1904–1964), the actor, was born Laszlo Lowenstein in Hun-
gary. He won early success in the German film *M* (1931). In 1934 he moved to
Hollywood and starred in such films as *Mad Love* (1935), *Crime and Punishment*
(1935), *The Maltese Falcon* (1941) and *Casablanca* (1942).

RICHARD MERRITT (B. 1921) was a photographic educator at the University of
New Hampshire (1970–1986) who directed many students to Jacobi Place. His
own work included color works in a variety of photographic media.

ERICH MÜHSAM (1878–1934) was an anarchist, poet, and playwright who was
sought out and murdered by the Nazis.

KARIN MICHALIS (1872–1950) was a Danish writer who had been published
by Erich Reiss Verlag and who helped to gain his release from a death camp.
After her work in Germany, she collaborated with Bertolt Brecht during his years
of exile in Denmark, 1935–1939.

TINA MODOTTI (1896–1942) was born in Italy and acted in the United States
in such films as *The Tiger's Coat* (1920). Her wide-ranging career encompassed

a trip to Mexico with Edward Weston in 1923. There she joined the Communist Party and practiced photography and political activism until 1930. She was in Berlin by 1930; Madrid in 1937, and Moscow in 1931. Refused admission to the port of New York in 1939, she returned to Mexico City. Long characterized as Weston's apprentice, Modotti is now recognized on her own artistic merits.

HELEN NEARING (1904–1995) established a home with her husband, Scott in Vermont (1932) and in Harborside, Maine (1951) in an effort to build a sustainable life based on revolutionary, practical ideas. Their homestead is now a retreat site.

SCOTT NEARING (1883–1983) was fired from the Wharton School for his opposition to child labor in 1915. He published *Living the Good Life: How to Live Sanely and Simply in a Troubled World* (1954), an expression of his lifelong goal to integrate economic, social, ecological and political concerns.

LOUISE NEVELSON (1900–1988), artist and sculptor, was born in Kiev, Russia. She traveled to Munich in 1931, and assisted Diego Rivera in his 1933 *Portrait of America* mural in New York. In 1986 she received the Guggenheim Museum Great Artist Series Award.

BEAUMONT NEWHALL (1908–1993) established the Department of Photography at the Museum of Modern Art in 1940. From 1958–71 he was the Curator of the George Eastman House in Rochester, New York. His survey text, *The History of Photography* (1949), is considered to be a classic.

NANCY NEWHALL (1908–1974) collaborated with her husband Beaumont on numerous books and exhibitions. In addition to this role, she was the principal editor of Edward Weston's *Daybooks* (1961).

ERICH REISS (1887–1951) was a progressive publisher during a retrogressive era in Germany history. He became Lotte's husband in America after escaping a death camp. For nearly a decade he collaborated with and published the plays of Max Reinhardt.

GARY SAMSON (B. 1951) directed the Jacobi Archives at the University of New

Hampshire from 1981 to 2001 and created *Lotte Jacobi: A Film Portrait* (1978). He is presently a faculty member of the New Hampshire Institute of Arts.

MAY SARTON (1912–1995) published fifty volumes, some with grants from the Guggenheim Foundation (1954–1955) and NEA (1967), notably *At Seventy: A Journal* (1984).

KURT VON SCHLEICHER (1882–1934) served as a general in the German army, led the transitional German government (1932–1933), and was murdered under direct orders from Hitler as part of the Rohm Putsch.

OTTO STEINERT (1915–1978) introduced the concept of *Subjektive Fotographie* through a 1951 exhibition. He worked as a photographer, curator and an educator in association with the Museum Folkwang, Essen, Germany.

ALFRED STIEGLITZ (1864–1946) edited *Camera Work* (1903–1917), and curated the 291 Gallery (1905–17), where he presented the work of Arthur G. Dove, John Marin, Marsden Hartley, and Georgia O'Keeffe, among others. He created a composite portrait of O'Keeffe (1917–1937) and introduced the concept of equivalence to photography.

ERNEST THALMANN (1886–1944) was the Communist candidate for the Reichspräsident (1932) in opposition to Hitler. In 1933 he was captured in Munich, served eleven years of solitary confinement, and was murdered at Buchenwald in August of 1944.

KARL VALENTIN (1882–1948) worked as a performing artist in Berlin.

KURT WEILL (1900–1950) was born in Dessau. His work as a composer included *Die Dreigroschenoper* (*The Threepenny Opera*, 1928). Despite his popularity with German audiences, Weill was censored in 1933 by the Nazi regime. He fled to Paris and then established himself in New York in 1935.

MINOR WHITE (1908–1976) in the tradition of Stieglitz, served as an editor, (*Aperture* Magazine, 1954–75), a curator (*Light 7* at MIT in 1968), a photographer (*Mirrors Messages and Manifestations* 1947–1968). He was a follower of Gurdjieff.

Dear Peter Moriarty,
Thank you for your letter of Dec 4.
I came back only a few weeks ago (End of Feb.)
to a lot of work. — If you would like to
come some times after next week, let me
know when you could. —
Kind regards,
Lotte Jacobi

March 13. 74.

Note from Lotte to the author on the verso
of the photogenic drawing shown on page 53

1. Moriarty, Peter. Lotte Jacobi interview. Deering, N.H., 22 November 1976. Rochester: Rochester Institute of Technology Library.

2. Ibid.

3. Moriarty, Peter. Beatrice Trum Hunter interview. Deering, N.H., 26 March 1996.

4. Ibid.

5. Ibid.

6. Moriarty, 1976.

7. Cohen, Selma Jeanne. *The Modern Dance: Seven Statements in Brief* (Middletown, CT: Wesleyan University Press, 1966), 77.

8. Ibid., p.86.

9. Jacobi, Lotte. *Lotte Jacobi: Theatre and Dance Photographs.* Introduction by Cornell Capa (Woodstock, VT: Countryman Press), 8.

10. Speer, Albert. *Inside the Third Reich* (Macmillan, N.Y., 1970), 422.

11. Moriarty, 1976.

12. Wheaton, Eliot. *Prelude to Calamity: The Nazi Revolution, 1933–35, With a Background Survey of the Weimar Era* (Garden City, N.Y.: Doubleday, 1968), 268.

13. Moriarty, 1996.

14. Moriarty, 1996.

15. Moriarty, 1976.

16. Ibid.

17. Moriarty, 1996.

18. Moriarty, 1976.

19. Ibid.

20. Ibid.

21. Ibid.

22. Sarton, May. Letter to Lotte Jacobi. 1962. Milne Special Collections. University of New Hampshire Library. Durham, NH.

23. Sarton, May. *At Seventy: A Journal* (Norton, N.Y., 1984)

24. Caponigro, Paul. Letter to Lotte Jacobi. 11 August 1966. Milne Special Collections. University of New Hampshire Library. Durham, N.H.

25. Caponigro, Paul. Sympathy note to Beatrice Trum Hunter. June 1980. Private Collection.

26. Carter, Jimmy. Letter to Lotte Jacobi. 14 September 1984. Milne Special Collections. University of New Hampshire. Durham, N.H.

27. Moriarty, 1976.

28. Mitchell, Margaretta. Bereavement note to Beatrice Trum Hunter. 12 June 1990.

29. Fern, Alan. Letter of condolence to Beatrice Trum Hunter. 11 May 1990.

30. Moriarty, 1976.

ACKNOWLEDGMENTS

Beatrice Trum Hunter supported the preparation of this manuscript through generous conversation and the loan of Jacobi family ephemera. Gary Samson and Lisa Nugent at the Jacobi Archives provided reproduction prints for this work. Joe Farara, chief librarian at Johnson State College, Laura Manzari, Diane Podell, and the entire reference department at C. W. Post searched for scholarly details. Jenny Studenroth assisted in creating a format for the text. Joanna Mayer introduced select passages from May Sarton. Bill Mitchell played Lotte Lenya recordings for me and suggested literature that was expressive of the Weimar era. Jean Osborne and Raine and Si Wapner provided warm meals and kindness throughout the project. Bill Ross and Roland Goodbody at the Milne Special Collection at the University of New Hampshire presented rare holdings from their Jacobi collection.

This book is dedicated to my family and to their embrace of the arts. My wife, Amy Beth is a movement therapist. Our children Mirah when dancing, Jacob while singing, Ella when acting, Jenny through designing, and Noah when playing cello have enriched my life.

PERMISSIONS

The author is grateful for the use of reproduction prints from the Lotte Jacobi Archives in the Dimond Library at the University of New Hampshire in Durham, New Hampshire. President Jimmy Carter and Paul Caponigro have approved quotations from their unpublished letters to Jacobi in the UNH Special Collections. Alan Fern and Margaretta Mitchell granted permssion to quote from their letters of condolence to Beatrice Trum Hunter, The University of New England Press has granted permission to quote from Selma Jeanne Cohen, *The Modern Dance: Seven Statements in Brief* (1965) and W. W. Norton and Company, New York, has permitted quotes from May Sarton, *At Seventy: A Journal* (1984.)

COLOPHON

LOTTE JACOBI has been set in Scala, a digital type designed by Martin Majoor in 1991. A distinctly contemporary face, Scala borrows the open proportions of old-style faces, the monoline strokes of geometric sans-serifs, and the slab serifs of so-called Egyptian faces. Indebted to no single family of types for its heritage, Scala succeeds (much like its distant cousin, W. A. Dwiggins's Caledonia) by virtue of its clean drawing, its vertical emphasis, its regular rhythm, and its somewhat casual letter forms. The display type is Penumbra, an multiple-master titling face of unusually handsome proportions designed by Lance Hidy in 1995.

Design and composition by Carl W. Scarbrough